Synod of Bishops

Rome, 1987

Instrumentum Laboris

The Vocation and Mission of the Laity in the Church and in the World Twenty Years after the Second Vatican Council

Office of Publishing and Promotion Services
United States Catholic Conference
1312 Massachusetts Avenue, N.W.
Washington, D.C. 20005-4105

ISBN 1-55586-165-2

CONTENTS

THE VOCATION AND MISSION OF THE LAITY
IN THE CHURCH AND IN THE WORLD
TWENTY YEARS AFTER THE SECOND VATICAN COUNCIL

INTRODUCTION

1. THE TOPIC

After seeking the opinion of the majority of Church institutions and in response to their requests, the Holy Father proposed for discussion at the Seventh Ordinary General Assembly of the Synod of Bishops the topic, "The Vocation and Mission of the Laity in the Church and in the World Some Twenty Years after the Second Vatican Council". As a result of the Second Extraordinary General Assembly of the Synod of Bishops, the regularly scheduled meeting and discussion of this topic was postponed from 1986 to 1987.

The proposed topic has a timely importance. Changes in contemporary society are occurring at a rapid pace and with far reaching effects. The laity, finding themselves in the very place where the interaction between the Church and the world is most visible and concrete, are simultaneously being called upon in a special way to accept their part in the Church's mission.

Twenty years after the conclusion of the Second Vatican Council, the Church rightly shares with ever greater conviction in the legitimate aspirations of individual persons and whole nations who are concerned about their dignity and freedom, either by seeking to protect them or by struggling to achieve them. But above all, the Church today is striving to understand Herself more perfectly and thus come to a clearer perception of Her vocation and mission. Undoubtedly, from this perspective the laity are a sign, source and cause of hope for the Church in these times.

Vocation and Mission are two distinct but inseparable aspects of one reality. The next meeting of the Synod will consider the interrelationship of vocation and mission as they apply to the laity. By seeking to understand the nature of the laity as fully as possible and

1

by seeking to properly define the task which the Lord Christ Himself has given them to do, the laity will be better able to exercise their part in the mission of the Church to make the gospel known to the world.

2. The Nature and Aim of the *Instrumentum Laboris*

On the basis of the *Lineamenta,* the purpose of which was to stimulate reflection in the local churches, there was an extensive consultation of the Church on this topic.

According to established custom, the General Secretariat of the Synod of Bishops diligently collected these reflections and considerations, sifted through them and drew up the customary *Instrumentum Laboris.* This document, then, presents the opinions which have resulted from a careful consideration of the reflections and responses of the *Lineamenta,* without, properly speaking, being a summary of their contents. However, the intent and purpose of the *Instrumentum Laboris* is not to present a comprehensive theology of the laity. It is clear that the foundations of such a treatment are amply presented in both the documents of the Second Vatican Council and of the magisterium accordingly set forth by the Supreme Pontiffs. This document, not intended to be a finished product, is proposed at the approach of the Assembly by the General Secretariat of the Synod as a kind of collection, resulting from an analysis of the reflections, experiences, suggestions and proposals received by the General Secretariat from the Synods and Episcopal Bodies of the Oriental Rites, from the Episcopal Conferences, from the Offices of the Roman Curia, from the Union of Superiors General of Religious and from other areas of Church life.

The topic chosen for the coming Synodal Assembly is of keen interest to the vast majority of the faithful, even if the very nature of the synodal assembly requires that it be the Bishops who treat and discuss the theme in its proper form. Nevertheless, the Holy Father has again granted permission, as he did for the Sixth Ordinary General Assembly on *Reconciliation and Penance,* to make the text of the *Instrumentum Laboris* available to the entire Church, even though it remains specifically intended for the members of the synodal assembly. Given the very special nature of the theme, the laity are encouraged to continue their reflection in a form and manner proper to each person's real life situation, bearing in mind the subject of the Synod.

3. An Overview of the *Instrumentum Laboris*

The *Instrumentum Laboris* is presented in three parts.

Part One: *The Contemporary Human Situation from the Perspective of Faith,* wishes to focus attention on the changes that characterize the present situation in society. Seen from the perspective of Faith such changes appear as a challenge to Christians on the occasion of a synodal Assembly devoted to a discussion on the laity whose situation in the world gives them a particular sensitivity in commenting on its process of development and a capability in being people of action for the Church's mission in the world.

Part Two: *The Laity and the Mystery of the Church,* primarily doctrinal in character, describes the exalted character of the vocation and mission of the laity. In light of the mystery of the Trinity, the laity by participating in the Church's vocation and mission help bring about the perfection of the work of creation through an application of the fruits of redemption. The sacraments, charisms and ministries are seen as those means of disposing the laity to grasping the true nature of their vocation and their call to holiness in the perfection of love, both of which point to the deep bond of *communio,* binding all the faithful in the Church, regardless of their state in life.

Part Three: *Witnesses to Christ in the World,* examines the forms, the places and the real life situations in which the laity, under the impulse of a deep spiritual life and programs for Christian formation, fulfill their vocation as true and proper collaborators in the Church's mission.

May the Spirit of the Lord, Who brings everyone together in the bond of *communio,* use this document as a stimulus to bring about within the Church at the approach of the Synodal Assembly a striving:

— "to clarify and deepen the understanding of the vocation and mission of the laity;

— to provide an answer, in *communio* with the whole Church, to present pastoral situations which are related to the involvement of the laity in the Church community and civil society;

— to support and encourage the laity to respond to their great potential, which results from their spiritual life and work in the apostolate, as well as to be of still greater service to the Church at this moment in history".[1]

PART I

THE CONTEMPORARY HUMAN SITUATION
FROM THE PERSPECTIVE OF FAITH

I.
THE DYNAMISM OF PARTICIPATION
IN TODAY'S WORLD

4. TWENTY YEARS AFTER THE COUNCIL

The present evolution of the world and the pressing questions which characterize recent socio-cultural changes impel the Church once again to take up—some twenty years after the Council—a reflection on the vocation and mission of the laity in light of the plan of salvation which God, in Jesus Christ, is accomplishing in history.[2]

The secular feature of the laity makes them indeed leading characters in the Church's mission in the world.[3] By their participation in the entire range of realities which make up the fabric of human existence, they realize this mission. Thus, by necessity they are involved in the complex working out of contemporary history.

Therefore the reflection on the "Vocation and Mission of the Laity Some Twenty Years after the Second Vatican Council" must view from the perspective of faith the human situation in which the laity live by reason of belonging to the Church. Such a perspective cannot fail to recognize that women and men are taking upon themselves a more active role through participation in contemporary society. This active participation is one of the distinctive characteristics of modern life.

5

5. PARTICIPATION AND PROGRESS

In looking at the past, the person of today realizes that the work and creative effort of previous generations have achieved for humanity a steadily-increasing dominion over nature and greater opportunity for more active involvement in the events of history. Today's men and women are aware of their capability to further improve the conditions of human life. At the same time, they witness in their own lives an increasing personal freedom. In this sense progress is seen to result from social involvement.

A strong movement of socialization has affected the intermediary structures of society: family, school, the world of work. All these have become places of cooperation among people and of continuous inter-action between persons and institutions. In many countries this process is just beginning, but not without a consciousness of its decisive importance. This point is powerfully emphasized in the traditional cultures of many people, where the participation of everyone in the life of the community has primordial importance.

The state of scientific and technological research gives reason for hope that the achievements of human intelligence will provide a basis for responding to the latest needs of humanity. While in some places living conditions do not correspond to the most basic needs of people, forcing them to suffer misery, the equitable redistribution of the world's resources appears as an imperative which can no longer be put off. For this reason, opportunity for participation must be urgently provided to the many who as yet stand on the periphery of the movement toward socio-cultural growth. At the heart of the universal human family the right of each individual is recognized to be a participant in the building of a personal and communal destiny.

6. THE POLITICAL DIMENSION OF PARTICIPATION

In many countries, participation in political life has considerably expanded and is presented even more as the duty of a civic conscience.

The political choices accomplished by women and men in real life situations, are the manifestation of an increased personal responsibility for the common good. In those cases where these decisions are expressions of a conscious and free choice there is a growing concern for the common good, bringing an appreciation for peace, justice, freedom, solidarity and fellowship.

The movement toward participation extends even beyond national frontiers and seeks to foster ever new international relations. There is a growing evidence of mutual initiatives of collaboration among people intended to lead to a more just political, economic and social order. New forms of exchange and dialogue at various levels are providing further opportunities for an international participation which favors a growing tendency toward mutual understanding and reciprocal assistance.

Today's men and women are conscious of being leading characters in a common destiny. This is expressed in the taking of positions and in the various forms of resistence in the face of the contradictions which more and more plague contemporary life, e.g., one part of humanity goes hungry while the other part, for selfish economic and political reasons, refuses to share its surplus of resources; the ever-present situations of violence and war, fuelled by the frantic race toward the production, selling and acquisition of arms.

A great many people living under totalitarian systems, oppressed by ideologies that restrict freedom and the right of participation are making urgent appeals for world solidarity. At the same time, group forms professing a doctrine of self interest are emerging at an alarming rate, tending to monopolize these areas of participation by denying them to others.

Among the many who are enjoying freedom there arises the need to become involved in denouncing totalitarian systems and demonstrating solidarity with those peoples who are suffering under such governments. Free people must inceasingly work in favor of all women and men in these times who have no other choice but to suffer passively under their political and authoritative power.

7. PARTICIPATION AND A CULTURAL IDENTITY

There is presently an increasing number of men and women who are aware that participation in the life of the community means the creation of a culture as well. The culture of a community is the expression of individual choices and common values. Culture, therefore, becomes an invitation for participation and dialogue between one person and another, between community and community.

Numerous initiatives from diverse areas of the social community are seeking to formulate new proposals aimed at making the living conditions of people more humane. These same initiatives at times clash with the opposing tendencies which limit the possibility of participating in the achievement and deepening of cultures.

While various branches of scientific knowledge become progressively more specialized and the diverse spheres of both individual and social life become even more independent, women and men likewise grow in a need for a cultural synthesis which is above all a synthesis of life. Where progress challenges the accepted patterns of life, it can likewise highlight their basic values. Therefore, there is a need to bring into harmony the richness of traditional cultures with a contemporary concern.

Today the mass-media and other forms of international communication are diffusing throughout the world a uniform culture, running the risk of limiting the areas of creativity for groups and communities. At the same time because of the unique contribution of the world dialogue between nations many people are rediscovering the meaning of their own cultural identity. Nevertheless, there is still the need to find adequate means for overcoming the disproportion in the opportunities of participation for various peoples and social groups in the benefits of culture. The participation of people in the life of society becomes at one and the same time the origin and expression of culture to the extent that they have the opportunity to communicate to others the values in which they believe and to share in the values lived by others.

8. PARTICIPATION AND THE DIGNITY OF THE HUMAN PERSON

Today participation at different levels of economic, social and political life has intensified interpersonal relationships, with the result that each person becomes aware of a responsibility to self and to others: the person discovers a unique dignity. At the same time each person realizes that such dignity brings with it precise ethical demands.

The varied and even contradictory circumstances in which women and men must live cannot stifle in their conscience that inclination toward good which is in the heart of each person that awakens a sense of dependence on a transcendent Good. Once the existence of God is acknowledged, the person is ushered into a life of interpersonal relationships and immersed in a basic awareness that the other person is entitled to an equal dignity.

The affirmation of the dignity and freedom of each person, the basis for the dynamic of participation, characterizes the life of a great many people in our day. However, in spite of this, many different forms of oppression against the dignity of the human person and whole peoples are increasing, demonstrating the urgent need for total liberation for all people.

The human person out of a sense of dignity for personal freedom, demands living conditions which will provide everyone with the opportunities and the means necessary to consciously participate in the life of national and international communities.

9. Participation and the Advancement of Women

The movement for the advancement and liberation of women is certainly one of the more significant manifestations of the general tendency toward participation. The just struggle in favor of recognizing the equality of rights between women and men at all levels, founded upon the assertion of their equal dignity, has not failed to bear fruit. Worthy of note are many positive results which have been accomplished by removing the obstacles which limited socio-cultural and political participation. In spite of this, the full recognition of the dignity of women—closely aligned to the question of the acceptance and affirmation of her feminine identity—is still a goal to be reached. In fact, when equality of dignity and rights between men and women was pursued in a purely formal way, resulting in the rejection of women's femininity, women found themselves faced with new experiences of oppression. A one dimensional emancipation, almost exclusively bound to the access of women to the economic world of production, has risked causing them to fall into a new state of alienation. When women are not part of the economic production system because they devote themselves to the family, they have had to face new denials to their dignity and their rights.

Furthermore, the actual prevailing culture tends to consider the roles of women and men as interchangeable at will, causing the reduction of the entire "being" and "acting" of a person to the pure, almost faceless, level of functionality. In studying the reactions to these new problems current thinking on women seems to have entered into a second phase. This thinking originates in the conviction that an affirmation of women's equal dignity requires a recognition of their differences also. The result is a rediscovery of the value of the complementarity between man and woman, who together are the total fulfillment of each other's humanity. From this perspective, marriage and the family are seen to signify the realization of this complementarity. Values, uniquely feminine, such as a particular sensitivity to the humane and to life, dialogue and communication, are today considered as an indispensable expression of the participation of women in the life of society.

10. OBSTACLES TO PARTICIPATION

No matter what their situation in life, women and men are involved in the mainstream of participation. However, the mentality directed to the temporal and the immediate, characterizing so many societies in which a good number of people live, does not always provide the possibility of participation which might serve authentic human development.

The mentality of secularism which eliminates God and the truths revealed by Him from the realm of the contemporary person, has changed the course of progress into an experience of insecurity and instability. Oftentimes, the lack of adequate ethical criteria leads to considering what is possible as the measure of what is permissible. Consequently, the fruits of progress become the threats of annihilation. The nuclear fear, the prospect of depleting natural resources, the outcry concerning ecological matters, the inherent risks of biogenetics, the questions that accompany the development of information systems are a cause for concern because of the ambivalence of progress.

Under the influence of a consumerism based on the philosophy of hedonism, women and men often limit their social participation to producing so as to possess and to possess so as to satisfy the desires of pleasure. There is no stopping this dynamic, not even when various forms of exploitation of the person become obvious.

Such experiences compel a search for new criteria of participation. The crisis in ideologies, undeniably a reality in our day, is very clearly calling the proposals of these systems into question, and it has simultaneously contributed to fostering a new sensitivity to the sacred. However, this renewed consciousness does not always lead to faith in a personal and transcendent God. Not a few women and men in their attempt to overcome the limitations of secularism are choosing the extremes of an easy mysticism or a religious fanaticism. On the one hand, the widespread existence of such phenomena points to the irrepressible sense of the sacred in the human heart, while on the other, it shows the Providential "appropriateness" of the Revelation of Christ which calls forth and fulfills this religious sense of the human person.

Looking at the contemporary situation from the perspective of Faith provides the opportunity to recognize to what extent the women and men of today are conditioned and determined by the dynamism of participation. Alone, however, men and women are unable to open the way that leads to self-fulfillment.

Therefore, while new possibilities and areas for participation are appearing, the search for meaning and self-fulfillment is growing as well. It appears, then, never more pressing and more timely than now, to bear witness to the truth that only Christ, Lord and Master, Key, Center and Purpose of all human history,[4] has the power to open the way to full participation for a person in the history of humanity.

II.
THE MISSION OF THE CHURCH
AND THE PARTICIPATION OF THE LAITY

11. FULL PARTICIPATION IN HUMAN HISTORY

The laity have the mission in the world in which they live to bear witness to the possibility of full participation in history according to the salvific plan of God.

Mary's "yes", which made the entrance of the Redeemer into history possible, signals the beginning of a new communion of the person with God and a more profound and universal unity of the human family. The Church is the sign and means offered to all of this extraordinary possibility for participation.

The person who is open to the gift of God in Christ, is open to a universal charity, which urges a person to share with everyone the spiritual and material resources given by God. Therefore, participating in the life of Christ in the Church means increasing the dynamism of participation that pervades human history and gives it unspeakable range.

12. The Advancement of the Lay State

From the beginning of Her history, the participation of the laity in the mission of the Church, in a variety of socio-cultural situations has represented one of the more significant dynamic means of heralding the invitation of full salvation in Christ. In the modern era, the great stages of the reawakening of the laity's responsibility to the mission of the Church, has to a great extent coincided historically with the rapid pace of scientific progress, the development of democratic culture and the emergence of new social problems resulting from the expansion of an urban-industrial civilization.

Nevertheless, such a reawakening was possible because the Church was simultaneously developing a profound self-awareness of Her Mystery and Her mission in the world.[5] In each flowering of mission activity in the Church resulting from this reawakening, many lay men and women were intensely involved as co-workers. In another sense, a major participation of the laity in Church tasks was manifested in the creation of new associations, important Christian institutions in the temporal order, and in a particular way, in the great current of Catholic social action.

These various forms of lay participation, developed in the last half of the 19th Century, as a result of a renewed responsibility of the Church in the world, merged in that broad movement for the advancement of the lay state, which, in its different forms of expression, is well able to be considered one of the great forces which prepared for the Second Vatican Council.

13. THE RESPONSIBILITY OF THE LAITY: NEW QUESTIONS

After the Second Vatican Council, there began a new season of lay participation in the life and mission of the Church. Many lay persons have become aware of the Church's unique responsibility to the world. Lay persons already know that they have the opportunity of making the Church present in the real life situations of human existence. They likewise understand that the failure to respond to this responsibility would mean a lessening of the Church's effectiveness in Her mission. The Bishops of the Church have encouraged this renewed consciousness, inviting the laity to participate in all areas touched by the Church's life and to bring to fulfillment the Christian presence in the world.

This state of affairs has sparked interest in new inquiries on the manner of living Church *communio* and responding to the needs of the world.

Much of the questioning taking place in the Church these days in view of the next Synod Assembly, can be conveniently grouped into two equally essential aspects of Church life:

a) a greater participation of the laity in Church *communio;*

b) a more effective presence of the laity in the Church's mission in the world.

Some questions are more concerned with a greater participation of the laity in Church *communio*:

— The increase of democratic participation in society makes many lay people, women and men, ask for similar participation in decision-making in the Church's life.

1. On what basis is participation in Church *communio* to be built?

2. What are the criteria for "representation" in the Church?

— A new flowering of associations characterizes the life of the laity in these days. A great many associations, groups and movements have been formed in the past few years on the provision of the right of free association in the Church.[5]

How are the charisms at the root of these and similar forms of association to be received and discerned?

How is the plurality of forms to be harmonized in view of the unity of Church *communio* and mission?

Other questions refer more directly to the mission of the laity in the contemporary world.

— The mentality of secularism deprives human existence of its true meaning and heightens the serious phenomena of disintegration. But a new search for personal meaning is indicatively manifested in the extreme forms of the return to the sacred.

In what ways can the laity bear witness to having found in the gospel of Christ a satisfying solution to the hungers of the human person?

In what ways are the laity, immersed in the world and yet bearers of faith and divine charity, able to do their part in overcoming this disintegration?

The laity are showing a new sensitivity when confronted with such phenomena as hunger, marginal people, war and every violation of human rights of individuals and whole peoples. They feel that these social contradictions can to a large extent be traced back to increasing numbers of materialistic systems and ideologies.

How can a person bear witness to the timeliness of the Redemption of Jesus Christ for constructing a more just world?

The Second Extraordinary Assembly of the Synod of Bishops, 1985 has already addressed some of these questions and by using the principle of Church *communio* has given a direction to theological and pastoral reflection on the matter.[6]

Such a principle provides the opportunity of composing a balanced synthesis of authority and freedom, personal responsibility and community participation, unity and plurality.

In light of what has been stated, the need now arises for a closer consideration of the vocation and mission of the laity in the Church and the world.

PART II

THE LAITY
AND THE MYSTERY OF THE CHURCH

I.
THE PARTICIPATION OF THE LAITY
IN THE VOCATION AND MISSION OF THE CHURCH

14. THE DISTINCTION BETWEEN VOCATION AND MISSION

The laity receive from God a vocation and mission in the contemporary human situation, the more important parts of which have been briefly described in the first part of this document.

Before actually treating the subject of vocation and mission as they appear twenty years after the Second Vatican Council, it is worthwhile to make a distinction between the two terms. Some, for example, use the words interchangeably with a certain indifference, saying that the *vocation* of the laity is to infuse the reality of the world with the Christian spirit or they refer to this as their *mission.* Where this manner of speaking is not incorrect, it does have the disadvantage of insisting on a one-sided relation of the laity to the world, to their role, or to their usefulness to the apostolic life of the Church. Seen in this way the laity run the risk of being considered simply as cogs in a huge complex. This agrees neither with the message contained in the New Testament nor with the insistence these days on the dignity of the human person, so often stressed by the Holy Father, Pope John Paul II.

The fact that the Second Vatican Council produced a decree *On the Apostolate of the Laity* does not mean that the apostolate is the only vantage point from which to define the place of the laity in the Church. Indeed, beginning from the Introduction, the decree understands a distinction between vocation and mission when it speaks of the apostolate of the laity as *ex ipsa eorum christiana vocatione promanans.*[7] Even though the apostolate is *derived* from vocation, it is not to be confused with it.

Vocation is broader than mission because it is composed of both a call to *communio* and a call to mission. *Communio* is the fundamental aspect destined to endure forever.[8] Mission, on the other hand, is a consequence of this call and is limited to an earthly existence.

15. CALLED BY GOD TO A *Communio* OF LOVE

Christians are *called* (*vocati*) by God to a personal relationship with Him in love. In our times the word *vocation* is frequently used without reference to the person who calls. This usage renders the term impersonal. The Bible, however, especially in the New Testament, insists on the initiative of a Person as the origin of a vocation. The One Who calls is God. The personal dignity of the laity arises predominantly from the fact that each one of them has been called by God Himself and invited to a personal relationship with Him. The New Testament when it addresses the faithful, refers to God as "Him who has called you" (*Gal* 1:16; *1 Peter* 1:15; 5:10) or "the one who calls you" (*1 Thess* 2:12; 5:24). It is important that the laity revive the awareness of this aspect of their vocation: God is interested in each one of them and has called each one of them.

The purpose of vocation is also personal, that is, God calls each one to a personal relationship with Him. He calls the laity "into His marvelous light" (*1 Peter* 2:9), "to his eternal glory" (*1 Peter* 5:10), "into the fellowship of His Son" (*1 Cor* 1:9), to "holiness" (*1 Thess* 4:7; *Rom* 1:6; *1 Cor* 1:2).[9]

The call comes from the Father, finds its expression in the mediation of Christ, that communicates the Holy Spirit to believers, thereby enabling them to respond fully to the divine call. Thus the Christian vocation is one of participation in the *communio* of love of the Holy Trinity.[10]

16. *Communio* IN THE CHURCH AND LIFE IN THE WORLD

Because it is a *communio* of love, such a vocation cannot be fulfilled in an individualistic manner. The call of the Divine Persons places all the faithful in a reciprocal relationship within Church *communio*. The vocation of every lay faithful, then, is to be rooted in the mystery of the love of Christ for the Church, which includes simultaneously, a personal aspect and a community aspect, inseparable from one another.

The love received and lived in this vocation by necessity has two dimensions: 1) a love for God which acknowledges that He has called and 2) a generous love for others, who are in union with God Who loves them.

In the Church, the ordained ministers are in service to this vocation, which the laity fulfill in the world, that is, in the real life situations of each human person (family, profession, social responsibilities, etc.).[11] The Christian vocation does not ask a person to flee from the world. In fact, "in all the Churches" (2 Cor 7:17) Saint Paul gave this exhortation: "So, brethren, in whatever state each one was called, there let him remain with God" (1 Cor 7:24). The doctrinal and spiritual teachings of many Saints (e.g. Saint Francis de Sales) give to this apostolic message, based on the presence of the Love of the Trinity in every human situation, a particular meaning for today.

17. GROWTH IN *Communio* WITH THE HOLY TRINITY

To grow in Church *communio* with God, the full gift of divine grace is offered to the laity, as manifested in *creation, redemption* and *sanctification.*

Participation in the work of creation is realized in the procreation and education of children,[12] and in another sense, through work, by which the person is able *opus Creatoris evolvere* [13] and to be united with Him.

The procreation and education of children associate a man and a woman to the Fatherhood of Him "from whom every family in heaven and on earth is named" (*Eph* 3:15).[14] Therefore, in the family the dignity of woman and man is manifested. In the family the basic fulfillment of the life of *communio* comes to be known as well.

In another sense, work in its varied forms, gives the lay faithful a special relation to creation. The human being created by God has received the mission to take dominion over the earth and all it contains.[15] Participation in the work of creation is realized through the responsibility of work which develops and perfects it.

Work is part of the Christian ideal of life. In one sense, it has a relation to the dignity of persons who, through work exert their power over the world. In another sense, Christians ought to recognize in work an essential form of witness to each other in love.

In the actual state of humanity after the Fall, family life and work have also become an opportunity for participation in the work of redemption. In fact, during the hidden life at Nazareth, family life and work constituted important aspects of the human life of the Son of God for the redemption of the world. Therefore, the dedication of the lay faithful in love and their application to work give them the opportunity to be united to the Redeemer.

Not only family and work, but all the aspects of human life, especially trials and sufferings, have become in Christ a means of redemption and provide the laity with valuable occasions to be united with Him in the work of redemption.[16] This is particularly true for the laity who live in countries where the Christian Faith is persecuted or opposed as a result of policies of discrimination, oppression and repression. In such circumstances Christians receive special graces which do not simply make a courageous endurance possible but also give the joy of blessedness [17] in virtue of their being united to the Passion of Christ.

Since redemption has resulted in the gift of the Holy Spirit for believers, the lay faithful are called to welcome the sanctifying action of the Spirit of God in all the circumstances of their lives. Their vocation is to become saints in all their conduct; [18] theirs is not a question of the common idea of holiness, achieved through a consecrated life apart from the world, but rather, of holiness through love and *communio,* according to the movement toward renewal set into motion by the Spirit of Christ.[19]

18. PERSONAL AND COMMUNITY MISSION

Because of the inseparable union of the two dimensions of Christian love, there corresponds to every vocation a mission. It is a question of the same vital movement which seeks to extend Church *communio* to all human persons, after the will of God, Who "desires all men to be saved" (1 Tim 2:4).

Mission consists in progressively transforming the world by means of a love that comes from God through faith in Christ.

Mission is entrusted to the Church. Its realization depends above all on the union of love which is to exist between the Christian faithful, itself a reflection of the divine *communio*.[20] Therefore, Church *communio* and mission are closely united.

Like vocation, mission, nonetheless, has a personal aspect. All the lay Christian faithful are to have a personal way of carrying out the mission of the Church according to their particular situation in the world: their human talents, their charisms, their responsibilities and the actual needs of the Church and the world at a given moment in time. This mission common to all is realized in a visible way through diverse "missions" carried out individually or in groups, permanent or periodic, among which some are acknowledged as ministries, even though the others are not necessarily less important.

The mission of the laity receives its specific character by their immediate involvement in worldly affairs. Nevertheless, it would be incorrect to make a distinction between ordained ministers and the lay faithful which might reserve to ordained ministers service to Church *communio* and to the lay faithful service to Church *mission*. It is true that the mission of authoritatively *preaching* the faith in the world is entrusted to ordained ministers, while the laity have the mission of *bearing witness* to the faith and of infusing all of human relations and the whole reality of the world with faith, hope and charity. However, in a mutual way, service to Church *communio* is likewise part of the vocation of the lay faithful. In this sense, their service is simply carried out in a different form from the sacramental service of the ordained ministers.

19. MISSION IN THE WORLD OF CREATION

To accomplish their mission properly, the laity have need of a working and balanced vision of the relation existing among the *Church,* the *world* and the *Kingdom of God*. These relations are not lacking in complexity. Therefore they require from the laity a sound capability for discernment.

Generally speaking, "world" is understood to mean the immense reality of creation which is fundamentally good [21] since it is the work of God. In facing the world the Christian has a positive attitude which receives with gratitude the gifts of the Creator, rejoices in the progress achieved in the area of human knowledge and in the human dominion over the universe and contributes to this through one's own work. The Church praises the Creator and proclaims the dignity of the human person, destined to "rule the world in holiness and righteousness" (*Wisdom* 9:3). With their varied activities the laity participate in this progressive dominion over the created world by humanity, while being especially attentive not to alter its equilibrium through disorderly activities or irresponsible destruction. Fully aware, however, that "here we have no lasting city" (*Hebrews* 13:14), the People of God do not limit their vision to the material organization of this world, but commit themselves to preparing for the final coming of the Kingdom of God, in which the world will be transfigured.[22]

20. MISSION IN THE HUMAN FAMILY

In a particular sense, "world" is understood to be the human world, that is, the whole of the human family. The mission of the Church, the "seed and beginning of the Kingdom",[23] is concerned more directly with this world and has the aim of making it more aware of its vocation to *communio* with God. The human world is the object of a redemptive love. "For God so loved the world that He gave His only Son, that whoever believes in Him should not perish but have eternal life" (*John* 3:16). According to the workings of redemptive love, the Church does not cease to open Herself to the world or to give of Herself so that all may become partakers of *communio* with the Father and the Son.[24]

The laity bring to the world the faith, hope and charity of the Church with a clear vision of the coming of the Kingdom. And they recognize with joy numerous signs of receptivity to the renewing action of the Spirit of God in the cultural and social developments of humanity.

21. MISSION AND THE MYSTERY OF EVIL

To receive redemptive love means also to recognize the existence of evil in the world and the necessity of a spiritual combat.[25] Our human world also manifests "the power of darkness" (*Luke* 22:53), subjected to the "ruler of this world" (*John* 12:31). The attitude of the Church toward "this world" cannot be positive. The Church cannot be a partner to darkness. Discernment is necessary to unmask false values and to denounce injustices, violations of human dignity and those things in opposition to the vocation to *communio* with God. Some twenty years after the Council the Church must face an ever stronger resistance by the world to accepting Christian values. On all sides one notices how much human history today is marked by processes contrary to restoring all things in Christ. The fruits of the human effort to take dominion over the world are appearing ambivalent. In such circumstances, the Church becomes a sign of contradiction, because She does not accept the easy principles of "this world". The Church's existence is identified with the mystery of the Cross.

The experience of living in modern society places many lay people under a tremendous tension between Christian values and the countervalues of the world. The result for them is two opposing temptations: to seek refuge in forms of religion without subtance, constituting a flight from the world; or to reject the demands of Christian faith in order to conform to a wordly existence.

On the contrary, fidelity to Christ and the Church demands a clearly visible witness. The Christian life must be presented courageously as an alternative to the values of "this world", that is, in its diversity according to the surrounding circumstances; not in a negative way of closing oneself off from it, but in the challenging perspective of an always open invitation.

In accordance with the mission of the Church, lay Catholics in sincere collaboration with other Christians,[26] as well as with all women and men of goodwill,[27] are working with trust and perseverance to nurturing all the seeds of good to be found in the world and are thereby contributing to the preparation of the complete realization of the Kingdom of God.

II.

COMMUNIO AND PARTICIPATION IN THE CHURCH

22. BAPTISMAL NEWNESS

Through Baptism all the faithful are immersed in the life-giving Mystery of Christ Crucified and Risen, thereby becoming members of His Body, the Church.[28] In the sacrament of Baptism, they indeed die with Christ to sin, that is, to a life according to their own will, and rise with Christ, to live no longer for themselves but for the Lord.[29] Having been conformed to the same Love of the Son for the Father through the action of the Holy Spirit in the Baptismal washing, the faithful commit themselves to remain in His love.[30]

Baptism, which opens the way to all the other sacraments, begins a New Life for the Christian, a Life which is qualitatively different from life according to the world.

To have only one Lord, one Faith, one Baptism is the foundation to the life of the chosen people of God; [31] as a result all its members possess the same Christian dignity.[32] The Baptismal character allows the faithful to participate in the Church's own vocation and mission, "Sacrament for the Salvation of the world".[33]

All the Christian faithful have the right to be educated to an awareness of their new beginning at Baptism.[34]

23. CONFIRMATION AND THE APOSTOLATE

Confirmation deepens the efficacy and effects of Baptism. The gift of the Holy Spirit endows the baptized person with a special strength, perfecting the person's bond to Church communio. Through Confirmation the faithful are particularly strengthened with a view to direct participation in the mission of the Church. In word and work they are called to bear witness to Christ and to spread and defend the faith.[35]

Therefore, in Confirmation participation of the faithful in the Church's vocation and mission is deepened.

Being called through the sacraments of Baptism and Confirmation to participate in the Church's mission in the world according to their real life situation, the lay faithful, on the basis of their union with Christ the Head, have the right/duty to the apostolate.[36] For this reason they can carry on the apostolic activity at their own initiative,[37] and also freely form and govern associations to promote the Christian vocation in the world,[38] as well as encourage such associations, provided they respect the duty of ecclesiastical Authority to oversee the exercise of the faithful's rights in view of the common good.[39]

24. THE EUCHARIST AND THE FULLNESS OF CHURCH *Communio*

In virtue of the Christian vocation the faithful participate in the Eucharist and draw from the fullness of Church *communio*: in the breaking of the bread they express their membership in the Body of the Lord and their membership with each other.[40] Only by being rooted in the Eucharistic memorial of the sacrifice of Christ and being continually orientated toward it, can the faithful make present and effective in the world the new life which comes from redemption.

"The Body of Christ (...) was but a grain of wheat, first falling to the ground and dying. Now, having undergone death, Christ abounds on our altars, made to bear fruit in our hands and in our bodies, and, while rising on high as the great and bounteous Master of the harvest, He gathers up with Him into the storehouses of heaven, this world in whose midst He became so great".[41] The Eucharistic memorial of the Passion is ineffective without a conversion of heart and the remission of sins, the first fruits of the blood shed by the Lord.[42] The Sacrament of Penance represents a most significant moment in which all the divine action of reconciliation is concentrated for the benefit of the faithful.[43] Without partaking of this action, the faithful cannot live the Eucharist as an authentic mystery of faith, capable of being the source and summit of their activities in the apostolate.[44]

25. PARTICIPATION IN THE *Tria Munera* OF CHRIST

The Sacraments of Baptism and Confirmation make the laity participants in the "three-fold office" of Christ, priestly, prophetic, and kingly, entitling them to live the mission proper to the People of God.[45] Participation in the three-fold office of Christ is fully exercised in the Eucharist, since the Eucharist establishes among all the members of the body of Christ that perfect bond of charity which is the soul of every action in the apostolate.[46] The *priestly office* makes the baptized a spiritual temple and a priestly people.[47] The laity are called to make an offering of themselves so as to bear witness to Christ everywhere. Through prayer, the sacraments, a holy life and above all, through charity, they live the common priesthood, which, while being different in essence from the ministerial priesthood endowed with sacred authority, is nonetheless, closely united to it, since both derive from the one and only priesthood of Christ. The common priesthood and the ministerial priesthood are in fact interrelated according to mutual correspondence, since the common priesthood continues to subsist in the ministerial priesthood, which in turn, exists and receives its justification from its service to the common priesthood.[48]

In virtue of the *prophetic office* the faithful, ordained ministers, religious and laity, which *in credendo falli nequit.*[49] For this reason the lay faithful never cease to enter ever more deeply into the mysteries of their faith through their daily lives, where, called by Providence to work, they witness to their faith, by announcing the gospel in word and work. In the contradictions of this present age, they write with patience—and not without suffering and struggle—the testament to their hope of eternal glory.

Until His glory is fully revealed Christ fulfills his prophetic office through all the Christian faithful: whether in a direct sense through the hierarchy who, by exercising their *munus docendi,* teach in the name of and with the authority of Christ, or, in an indirect sense, through His witnesses, the laity, whom He provides with the appreciation of the faith (*sensum fidelium*) and the grace of the word.[50]

Through the *kingly office* the laity participate in the action in which the Risen Lord is drawing all things to Himself in order to subject them, along with Himself, to the Father so that God be all in all.[51] Because of their special place in the world the laity are called to accept the value of creation, and supported by grace to relate it to God through their various activities. In this way the world will be transformed by the Spirit of Christ, the Spirit of justice, charity and peace.[52]

26

The participation in the kingly office proper to all the lay faithful and that of the hierarchy, though different in essence because of the *sacra potestas,* are intimately correlated. This fact should foster in the Church a deep family relationship between the Bishops and the Laity.[53]

26. Mary, Model for the Believer and for the Dignity of Woman

"Hail, O Mary, because you had subject to you the One who rules heaven and earth!
Hail, O Mary, Morning Star heralding the Sun of Eternal Day!
Hail, O Mary, Fruitful Mother of a new creation!".[54]

Through her consummate "yes", in response to God's initiative for the salvation of humanity, reaching even to the Cross, Mary participates in a singular way in the *three-fold* office of Christ.[55]

By welcoming in perfect faith the Incarnation of the Son of God into this world, by living out the mysteries of her existence in a continuing relationship to the Saviour, and by humbly submitting to worldly affairs, beginning with the hidden life of Nazareth, Mary has become the model of every Christian.[56] Her singular vocation witnesses to the greatness of the life of the lay person, called to participate in redemptive power through a free and personal acceptance in grace.

Mary's exalted position characterizes the life of the entire People of God and points the way towards reconsidering the value of women in the Church and provides a means of avoiding within the Church the inequality from which women suffer in society. In the Christian community Mary shows the way towards affirmation of the equal dignity of man and woman in the variety of their charisms and services. The place of Mary in the Church exalts the significance of femininity as opposed to lessening the image of woman in the attempt to abolish every difference and element of her complementarity to man.[57] It is impossible to forget that Mary, woman of the people of Israel, has become the crowning point of the holiness of humanity.

27. The State in Life of the Laity

Participation in a specific manner in the three-fold office of Christ, begun in Baptism and strengthened in Confirmation and fully exercised in the Eucharist, serves as the basis for the Church vocation and mission of every lay person.[58]

From this perspective it becomes clear that the Christian's state in life, as such, provides the link to the Mystery of Christ Himself, lived so fully by the person of Mary. Saint Paul says that the distinguishing content of the state in life of each believer is *living Christ,* that is, to be Christian.[59]

Thus the state in life of the lay Christian faithful is seen to have common ground with the rest of the Christian faithful since each person's state in life is the basic element shared by all the People of God. For this reason, the states in life of the bishop and the religious are themselves related to specific conditions which derive respectively from the Sacrament of Orders and from the Consecration in the evangelical counsels.

Such a "personalizing" of the state in life of the laity is unable to have as a consequence either the marginalization or the clericalization of the character of the lay person. This fact is supported by the very existence of a manifold variety of charisms, tasks and ministries among the People of God.[60] These words point to an undeniable richness in the Church. They are also an incentive for the laity to assume a distinct personal responsibility within the structure of the Church Body.[61]

28. THE LAITY IN THE WORLD

The Church's approach in mission is directed to "the total salvation of the world".[62]

In this work the lay faithful occupy a privileged place that gives them the opportunity to participate in an essential way in the overall vocation and mission of the Church.

The secular character of the laity allows them to accomplish in a special way the salvific mission of the Church in the world, bearing witness to their belonging to Christ, while dealing with temporal things.[63] While always seeking the Kingdom of God, they strive to relate the things of the world to God, and by living up to their responsibilities in this age, consequently, they cause their faith, hope and charity to shine forth.[64] Aware of the relationship between human and salvation history, which can be explained only in light of the Paschal Mystery, the laity are called not only to cultivate but defend all authentic human values, maintaining all the while the necessity of further purifying and elevating these values by the grace of the Spirit of the Lord, in view of total salvation.[65] The Church's mission must not indeed be reduced to its spiritual aspect and even less—in the opposite extreme—to a purely temporal one. This mission "though spiritual, involves also human advancement in the temporal area".[66] Thus, the distinction between the natural and supernatural aspects, necessarily involved in this mission, can never become separated and its dual aspects are never able to become a dualism.[67]

For these reasons the laity are to strive to overcome the pernicious separation between professed faith and daily life, by allowing themselves to be always guided solely by a Christian conscience in the spiritual and the temporal matters in which they are simultaneously engaged.[68]

29. THE MARRIED STATE

Marriage gives a particular importance to the state in life of the majority of the laity.[69] It indeed confers on the lay state a supernatural character in a manner which is not attainable in other states. In fact, Christ brought to fulfillment the marriage of Eden, raising it to the dignity of a sacrament, patterned after the mystical relationship between Christ and the Church.[70] The love between Christ and His Church thus becomes the point of reference for married love, which gives to the life-giving mystery of human generation the spiritual fruitfulness of faith, hope and charity.[71]

Since the family is the domestic Church,[72] then the intimate *communio* of life and love,[73] the relationship of husband and wife, of paternity and maternity, of offspring and fellowship which are born in it, ought to become the aim of the laity's mission.

Christian faith is indeed called to permeate these relationships so that they might be able to transform with every passing day the tenor of daily life and to proclaim to all the world the power of the Kingdom of God and the hope of the Christian life.[74]

30. THE MANIFOLD RICHNESS OF CHARISMS

Through the Holy Spirit the life of the faithful in the Church is continually being enriched by charisms, tasks and ministries. "The Holy Spirit apportions His charisms to each one individually as He wills" (*1 Cor* 12:11). These are special gifts, sometimes extraordinary, sometimes very simple. In describing and classifying these gifts the New Testament texts reveal their great variety.[75] Nevertheless, all seem to show that the grace expressed in each of them always involves a task to accomplish.[76]

In regard to unity within diversity, all those who have received charisms have the right/duty to exercise them both in the Church and in the world for the good of humankind and the building up of the Church.[77] Many of these charisms are given to the laity, who in turn are called to use them with the freedom of the Spirit Who blows where He will (*John* 3:8).[78]

The extraordinary charisms cannot be asked for imprudently or with presumption;[79] and in any case, no charism dispenses a person from the jurisdiction of the Bishops in the Church.[80] In effect, judgment on the genuineness of the charisms and their related use is the task of ecclesiastical Authority to which "above all, belongs the task of not extinguishing the Spirit"[81] but rather of retaining what is good, so that all the charisms may work together for the common good.[82]

31. TASKS AND MINISTRIES

The charismatic action of the Spirit is also linked to the rise of ministries in the Church.

Concerning the non-ordained ministries of which the Council has already spoken[83] the Supreme Pontiffs Paul VI[84] and John Paul II[85] have strengthened and broadened them on both a doctrinal and pastoral level. In particular, they have taught that the non-ordained ministries are to be entrusted to the laity so that their exercise might be seen as a sign of the greater vitality of the Church community.[86]

In singling out and co-ordinating the non-ordained ministries, the special place of the laity in the world must not be forgotten. If respect for their secular character is kept in mind, the grave danger of clericalizing the laity will be diminished.[87]

32. THE NEED FOR CLARIFICATION REGARDING THE NON-ORDAINED MINISTRIES

The exercise of the non-ordained ministries entrusted to the laity requires careful consideration. It seems necessary to define the difference between the tasks commonly assumed by the laity and those of ordained ministries. This distinction will be possible only after having outlined the essential connotations and characteristics of Church ministry entrusted to the laity.

Furthermore, it will be necessary to address a series of questions which are of relative importance:

— Who can authorize the creation of such ministries in the Church?

— What ought to be the manner of entrusting the laity with non-ordained ministries? (A liturgical rite or simply by a juridical act?)

— What ought to be the duration of such ministries and the manner of discontinuing them?

33. *Communio* AND CORRESPONSIBILITY OF THE THREE STATES OF THE CHRISTIAN LIFE

The relationship among the three state of life, without entering into the doctrine of the Council of Trent [88] on the pre-eminence of the virginal and celibate states, is one of reciprocal correspondence. In a certain sense, it can be said that the lay state in life is the state to which the other two states are ordered; but it must likewise be acknowledged, from other points of view, that the other states are in turn, ordered to the presbyteral state or to the religious state.

Indeed, the states in life receive their deep significance in relation to the perfection of love, the common goal of all the faithful. For this reason the one exists for the other.

In this respect each state in life fully accomplishes what is also essential for the other two. The presbyteral state represents the permanent guarantee of the sacramental presence of Christian redemption in every place and time. The religious state bears witness to the demand of absoluteness intrinsic to the "duty of being Christian" which urges each of the faithful to bring together as far as possible "what I am" and "what I ough to be". Finally, the lay state leads to the sanctification of all human conditions in *communio* with the Trinity.

This reciprocal correspondence within the Church *communio* is the proper foundation for mutual edification and for the Church responsibility held in common by the three states in life, so that, in proper relationship and distinctions, all might visibly bear witness to the charity of Christ and to the Holiness of God: "For this is the will of God, your sanctification" (*1 Thess* 4:3). Indeed, before God the degree of holiness does not depend on the state in life, but on the perfection of charity.

PART III

WITNESSES OF CHRIST IN THE WORLD

I.
LIFE ACCORDING TO THE SPIRIT

A) *DISCIPLES OF CHRIST*

34. UNITY OF LIFE

In providing the basis for the new influx of the laity into the Church's mission in the apostolate, the replies to the *Lineamenta* emphasized the necessity of overcoming the separation of faith from life.

The reflection of the Seventh Ordinary General Assembly of the Synod of Bishops begins the work of determining the ways in which every lay person might come to know how to insert in a Christian synthesis all the realities of their human existence.[89]

Only in this way will the Christian be able to show others the path that leads to true freedom and true peace.

This witness of the faithful is fulfilled in a plurality of forms, personal and communal, inspired by the Spirit, in the everyday conditions of life.

35. THE UNIVERSAL CALL TO HOLINESS

The universal call to holiness in charity as taught by the Second Vatican Council must be at the heart of the spiritual life of every believer.[90] Such a call requires overcoming the unjust separation of faith from life. Indeed, the fullness of charity implies wholeness. No aspect of daily life, therefore, can remain separated from its dynamism which seeks the glory of the Trinity and the total good of humanity.

The mystery of the Incarnation of the Son of God—Who became man out of love for humanity—reveals that in the life of Jesus nothing was unrelated to his salvific mission. Every aspect of His existence, e.g., His life in a family, His work in the obscure village of Nazareth, had a redemptive meaning. Therefore, the entire daily life of the lay faithful must be viewed as part of the salvific plan of the Father which is brought to completion through the Spirit.

36. THE "FOLLOWING OF CHRIST"

The need arises, then, for a newness of life. It is no longer possible to live in the world as those who have not known the Lord.[91] Those who have known Him must act like Him.[92] Christ fulfilled His work of redemption through loving submission to the will of the Father, "He humbled Himself and became obedient unto death, even death on a cross" (*Phil* 2:8). Therefore, He offered that sacrifice through which we too have been made holy.[93]

To conduct oneself like Christ—to follow Jesus—every lay person is called above all to renounce any sinful relationship with the world for love of the Father. Furthermore it demands that a person's existence must be lived in the spirit of obedience to the Father's plan of salvation in Christ.[94]

37. THE NECESSITY FOR DISCERNMENT

In every stage of history the plan of salvation is fulfilled with different features which correspond to the current needs of the human family. These are the signs of the times, which for the disciples of Christ are not simply an incidental change in historical conditions and even less are they behavioral standards for the Christian to follow. Instead, they are current and clear calls from God for a more concrete Christian response.

Consequently the laity cannot withdraw into an individualistic search for God, but must commit themselves to respond to the current needs of the world: "for he who does not love his brother whom he has seen, cannot love God whom he has not seen" (1 John 4: 20). To have an authentic spiritual life, the Christian must be able to discern through faith the voice of Christ who is calling even today in the aspirations and expectations of people. Attuned and sympathetic to the needs of humanity,[95] the Christian is always to be ready to respond to them by seeking new and old solutions to problems.

38. A Life Style according to the Beatitudes

Christian service to others requires the gift of oneself in everyday existence.

Therefore, "He laid down His life for us; and we ought to lay down our lives for the brethren" (1 John 3: 16). This fundamental attitude is translated into a life style according to the Beatitudes, proclaimed by Jesus and expressive of the perfection of a gospel love.[96]

The laity follow Christ Who Himself was poor. Therefore, they do not lose heart at the lack of temporal goods, nor do they give way to pride in times of abundance. Untiringly they seek the justice of God, the basis for true peace among people.

For justice's sake they are willing to suffer persecution, while renouncing every type of violence. In the passion of Christ they find the strength to overcome the trials of existence, and in His resurrection, an inexhaustible source of joy and hope.[97]

B) *GROWTH IN THE LIFE OF GRACE*

39. A Continuing Conversion

Just as the Kingdom of God is a small seed that grows gradually until it becomes a big tree able to accommodate the birds of the sky,[98] so the growth of charity in the Christian gradually integrates all the dimensions of human existence, placing them in the service of God and of humanity. In this way the conversion of the Christian brought about in Baptism does not remain an isolated event of the past, but becomes a continuing process of breaking from evil and of growth in remaining close to Christ.

Not every tendency opposed to the Reign of Christ in the human heart is immediately identifiable. What is needed is the patient work of discernment, of conversion and of struggle. On the other hand, the heart must have charity as its total life by constantly opening itself to the gifts of the Spirit and by a true development of the Christian virtues.

40. THE WORD OF GOD

Through the Word of God, proclaimed in the Church's Liturgy and meditated upon in a person's life, the Father Who is in heaven enters into conversation with His children [99] and makes the human heart able to know the mystery of His saving will. In this way those aspects of a personal life that require conversion are brought to light and the vast horizons for transforming the world are opened.

The Word of God is a "pure and perennial source of the spiritual life".[100] Its message, always current, illuminates the events of human history, preparing the mind and heart of people to receive from the Spirit a new light for their personal destiny and the history of humanity. Furthermore, meditating on the Word of God, the laity learn to judge correctly the true meaning and value of temporal realities.[101] The growing familiarity of the laity with the Word of God is an irreplaceable element in their spiritual life.

41. THE EUCHARIST

The Eucharistic Sacrifice, *totius Vitae Christianae fons et culmen,*[102] must occupy the central place in the lives of the laity. It is here that they actively participate both in the actual Eucharistic celebration and in their daily life, offering to God the Father the whole of their earthly day in a union of love with the sacrifice of Christ.

In the Eucharist, Jesus Christ proposes to the faithful the perfect model of charity and communicates salvation, giving Himself as the food of eternal life. In this way the Eucharist effects a detachment from egoism and urges a living of *communio* as a criterion for every activity.

The everyday life of the laity acquires an authentic meaning only in remaining united to the Eucharistic Sacrifice. There it reaches its fulfillment since in the Eucharist Christ unites to His own offering whatever good the members of His Body have accomplished.[103]

42. COMMUNAL AND PERSONAL PRAYER

Prayer, both communal and personal, is essential to the sanctification of the Christian.[104] Through prayer those who look to the Trinity as the source of every good, have their hopes realized; they seek spiritual and material help and give thanks for their constant blessings.

In praying the Christian ought to be identified with the prayer of Jesus Christ, since it is only "through Him we both have access in one Spirit to the Father" (*Eph* 2: 18).

In this union with Christ the Christian is able to pray to the Father with the sincerity and faith characteristic of the person who knows he is a child of God. After the example of Christ, Who in prayer submitted His entire life to the saving plan, the faithful offer themselves to the Father so that His Plan might be realized in the personal and community circumstances of their lives. Furthermore they ask for the grace and strength of the Spirit so that the same will of the Father may be fulfilled in them.

43. RECONCILIATION IN SACRAMENT

Since the People of God on earth are *in membris suis peccato obnoxius,*[105] the faithful if they are to be converted, must confess their sins with a contrite heart in the Sacrament of Penance.[106]

Furthermore this sacrament is a source of hope until the last day of existence on the earth,[107] since God the Father finds His lost child there and restores a dignity previously had.[108] The Christian is thus able again to respond to the vocation to *communio* and mission with a deeper awareness of personal weakness and with a greater conviction of the divine mercy.

Through the frequent practice of sacramental confession, Christians are able to purify all the aspects of their conscience that are still subject to the frailty of sin. Then the grace of the Holy Spirit will more clearly be manifested in every aspect of the life of Christ's followers, and through them the face of the Lord will be made more visible for all people to see.

44. CHRISTIAN ASCETICISM

The positive reply to God's call is to be confirmed in the deeds of everyday life, since "not every one who says to me, 'Lord, Lord', shall enter the kingdom of heaven, but he who does the will of My Father Who is in heaven" (Matt 7:21). Therefore, the laity ought to practice in their lives a courageous asceticism,[109] proceeding with the help of the Spirit per viam fidei vivae, quae spem excitat et per caritatem operatur.[110]

Their ascetic commitment ought to be applied to the social aspects of their everyday life, correcting the defects that are an obstacle to family peace and nourishing the spirit of collaboration at work and their availability for service in the Church and civil community. In this regard the virtues that concern social justice, such as prudence, honesty, the spirit of justice, sincerity, courteousness and fortitude are all important.[111]

45. MARY, MOTHER OF THE SPIRITUAL LIFE

After Christ, the perfect model of all spiritual life is the Blessed Virgin Mary quae, dum in terris vitam ageret omnibus communem, familiari cura et laboribus plenam, intime semper cum Filio suo coniungebatur et operi Salvatoris singulari prorsus modo cooperata est.[112] In listening to and meditating on the Word of God, in participating in the Eucharist, in prayer, in penitence and in the spiritual struggle, the laity are to place their trust in her protection since materna sua caritate de fratribus Filii Sui adhuc peregrinantibus necnon in periculis et angustiis versantibus curat, donec ad felicem patriam perducantur.[113]

II.

THE PERSONS ENTRUSTED WITH MISSION

A) *PARTICIPATION OF ALL THE FAITHFUL IN THE CHURCH'S MISSION*

46. THE CHURCH IN THE MISSION STATE

By Her very nature the whole Church is "mission-ary". Furthermore today Her mission task is so immense and decisive that it calls for the participation of all the faithful. Renewing the bonds of *communio* and apostolic zeal, all are called to cooperate *ad dilatationem et incrementum Regni Christi in mundo.*[114]

In this regard the teachings of Vatican II, received and put into practice, have produced obvious fruit both in older and younger Churches.

The Church has become more fully aware of the laity's Christian dignity and their responsibility in the apostolate. The laity's participation in the mission of the Church has increased and become more varied.

Nevertheless, in many Churches the laity who are indeed conscious of their dignity, and above all, are involved in the mission activity in the various fields of their daily life are still a minority. Too many are passive and confine their association to Christianity to ritual moments. It must also be mentioned that a "clericalism" sometimes aids this state of affairs.

To place the entire Church in a "mission state" requires an enthusiasm for a new evangelization that might spread to all the baptized faithful.

47. EVANGELIZATION AND INCULTURATION

Ten years from the conclusion of the Second Vatican Council, at the close of the Third Ordinary General Assembly of the Synod of Bishops, *Evangelii Nuntiandi,* set in bold relief the nature of mission activity, stating that evangelization expresses the profound identity of the Church Herself [115] and forms the essence of Her mission. To bring the Good News to all levels of humanity, to bring about a change in the criteria of judgment, normative values, interests, ways of thinking and patterns of life, means opening to the world and to all people the road that leads to complete salvation.

Twenty years after the Council, the Second Extraordinary Assembly of the Synod thoroughly examined the dynamics of "inculturation" of the Gospel. In virtue of the principle of *communio* which is capable of blending a diversity into a unity, the Church, without reverting to easy exterior conformity, is in a stage of welcoming in a profound way those elements that She encounters in every culture, to assimilate them and integrate them into Christianity, and to root the Christian way in different cultures. [116]

The evangelization of culture and the "inculturation" of the Gospel are intertwined in the Church's mission task and involve Her in a real sense in the construction of a civilization of truth and love.

48. HOPE FOR MISSION

Within the framework of the participation of all the faithful in the mission of the Church, the Second Extraordinary Assembly wished to give prominence to young people and to women.

Young people, who have need for statements of substance and lofty ideals, represent a living incentive for the Church's mission. At a time in which they are faced with ever greater difficulties—in the world of work because of unemployment, in school through a shortage of "teachers" and the lack of certain criteria for truth—and are tempted by hedonistic conformism or by old ideologies, the Church invites them to receive and energetically continue the legacy of the Council. On the threshold of the year 2000, the growing participation of young people in the mission of the Church—in groups, communities, movements—is a sign of hope for the entire People of God.

The Church has always shown a great love and deep respect for children, following the words of Christ. They have the right to a familial atmosphere—both in society and in the Church—to allow them to grow not only in age but in wisdom and grace.[117] They are bearers of the profound values of life for the mission of the Church and in the building of a more humane world.

Also the participation of women in the life and mission of the Church is often more vast and committed than that of men. The Church wishes to avoid every discrimination with regard to the dignity of all the laity —women and men—promoting *communio* in their proper mission. To acknowledge and promote the gifts and the responsibilities of women so that they might participate more fully in the activity of the Church in Her different tasks in the apostolate[118] is a need that is particularly felt in the entire Church body.

49. The Poor in the Church's Mission

The Church, which is, and wishes more and more to be, the home and family of God, open to all, receives the poor with a preferential love. She has become ever more aware of Her mission in their service according to the true spirit of the Gospel, and in listening to the cry of millions of people in need and in expectation of a true liberation, She especially makes Her own their joys and sorrows, their anxieties and their hopes.[119] With them, She senses the deep bonds of *communio* and solidarity. Those who suffer from poverty and hunger, the oppressed, the abandoned, the emarginated, those who suffer from physical or psychic infirmities, participate in a uniquely special way in the Cross of Christ and therefore in the Church's mission.[120]

B) THE OUTLOOK OF THE FAITHFUL IN THE MISSION TASK

50. Necessary Attitudes

Some attitudes essential to a Christian conscience and practice characterize the participation of the laity in the mission task of the Church. Without them it is impossible for the Christian to bear active and fruitful witness to his identity whenever the life of a person and the destiny of peoples might be at stake. These attitudes are an indispensable condition if the laity are to promote, in every human situation, that process of inculturation of the faith which, by virtue of their secular character, they are called to fulfill with a particular commitment.

51. SHARING AND SOLIDARITY

There is nothing genuinely human that does not find an echo in the heart of Christians.[121] The attitude which includes a love towards every person, a desire to share in the surroundings of every human life, of rooting in every culture, of a passionate concern for the destiny of one's own people, a human solidarity which knows no limits, are signs of receptivity for the Christian presence. In fact, humanity is "always" the way of the Church [122] in the diversity of situations, of needs and of deep expectations, in the search and discovery of the personal meaning of life, in the anxious quest for truth, justice, peace and happiness.

52. JUDGING LIFE IN A CHRISTIAN MANNER

To be present in everything that is authentically human requires an ability to judge all the events of life in light of faith in Christ. Christ reveals one person to another and manifests to each, a unique vocation, dignity and goodness.[123] Christ is the touchstone to all human experience.

The Christian judgment on reality teaches a discernment of the signs of truth, of goodness and of beauty present in every human situation. The Christian presence must assume them and elevate them.

At the same time the Christian judgment denounces every form of oppression, of manipulations and alienation. It makes a person see that sin is at the root of every division and slavery, and urges the laity to devote themselves to a practice of Christian liberation.[124]

53. A "Forthright" Witnessing

Announcing and witnessing to the Good News requires from Christians an attitude of forthrightness (*parresia*).[125] Wherever they live they are obliged to manifest in words and in action, the "new man" with whom they have been clothed in Baptism and the gifts of the Holy Spirit received in Confirmation.[126] *Parresia* often endows the Christian witness with a particularly captivating quality which evokes a wonder in others at the depth of goodwill with which believers are able to give an "account for the hope that is in you" (*1 Peter* 3:15).

54. Building with Christian Realism

The laity are to commit themselves to the real life situation in which Providence has placed them, so as to order and transform the world according to the values of the Kingdom of Christ. They are to be leading characters in building a world of greater justice, peace and solidarity. But, at the same time, they must not forget the essential fragility nor the ambivalence always present in every human situation. With an attitude of Christian realism they are to aim for effectiveness in history with the conviction that every good deed will reach fulfillment in Christ. This authentic "poverty of spirit" is to convert them into bearers of active hope, which surpasses every utopian dream. For the Lord of history will in fact manifest "a new heaven and a new earth" in the final liberation, which is at work even now among people.[127]

55. In Dialogue

The *communio* of Christians in every real life situation—district, school, office, factory, hospital...—makes the Church present in a dialogue with whomever She comes in contact.[128] This dialogue is to make the laity particularly conscious above all of their responsibility to ecumenism. In fact the concern of restoring unity among Christians touches each person according to one's own capacity. In the environment in which the laity are called to speak, they are to make reference to the common gospel heritage, aware that the responsibility to witness often requires Christian to work together.[129]

In their mission activity, the laity are to be aware that non-Christian religions possess a spiritual heritage of great importance, on which the gospel must be grafted. An authentic witness of life knows how to bring out the value of religious feelings present in other believers without renouncing the demands of the Gospel.[130]

In conclusion, by engaging in dialogue with those who seem to be indifferent to God or who have strayed from Him, the laity are to testify that the questions essential to human existence (the meaning of life and death, of suffering and work, of joy and love...) demand an all-inclusive vision of the good of humanity, the foundation of which can only be found in God.[131]

Lay believers are to work together with Christians of other confessions and with people of good conscience and good will, on every possible occasion, yet without ideological compromises, in order to create a way of life that is more worthy of the person.[132]

C) IN COMMUNIO FOR MISSION

56. THE LAITY AND THE MISSION OF THE LOCAL CHURCH

The laity live their incorporation in the one universal Church in "local Churches" which make the "Catholic Church" present in different places.[133] The joint responsibility of the laity to participate in the needs and pastoral programs of a diocese involves them in Her mission endeavors. The mission dimension lived in a concrete manner has caused more familiar relationships to develop within the community and particularly among Bishops.

Without prejudice to the specific pastoral responsibility of ordained ministers, the laity are presently participating to a greater degree in the decision-making processes of the Church.

In an institutional sense, pastoral councils have helped to encourage and guide this renewed community dynamic of dialogue and collaboration among the faithful. Recommended by the Council itself,[134] it is desirable that their creation and their employment should become more general in the local churches. To be in service to *communio* and the overall mission, the laity must, in many cases, overcome some obstacles which have commonly characterized this first phase of their existence: an over emphasis on the organizational and bureaucratic aspects to the detriment of the mission outlook; strong tensions on questions of "representation" within the local Church; continuous wavering between "clericalism" and "false democracy".

Deserving of special attention are the experiences resulting from a greater participation of the laity in the life of the local Church, in diocesan and national assemblies or at Synods.

57. THE LAITY AND THE MISSION OF THE PARISH

The Parish continues to be the usual place of participation by the laity in the Church's life and mission. In parishes they discover and constantly live their character as People of God, participating in the divine mysteries through a renewed liturgical and sacramental life.[135]

In the last 20 years the institution of the Parish pastoral council, promoted by Vatican II, has been followed in Parishes by a flourishing of initiatives that have stimulated the aspect of the mission of the laity: a liturgical and community involvement; various schools of catechesis (pre-sacramental catechesis, the catechesis of children, of young people, of families; the Rite of Christian Initiation for Adults...); charitable programs, voluntary services, the promotion of humanitarian goals within a given territory, groups of cooperation in mission and other activities.

Yet in many situations a great number of believers limit themselves to a passive presence in the liturgy and the sacraments with the result that the parish is not able to come together as a true force in the community, capable of a real zeal in service to the demands of mission.

The need for more intense personal and community relationships among the faithful and a greater participation in the life and mission of the Church has caused many to form "small Christian communities" or "basic Church communities". Sometimes in Parishes which cover large areas or in other cases in densely populated areas where the institutional presence of the Church is still fragile or only just beginning, such experiences have helped the realization of the Church's mission by meeting the personal needs of people. The Church criteria of discernment, concerning this new manner of the faithful's "*communio* and participation" in building up the Church have been stated by the magisterium on several occasions.[136]

In this context the irreplaceable work of catechists for the initial and continuing evangelization of different countries cannot be forgotten. With competence and dedication they have reached their twofold objective: to nurture the faith and to become the point of contact between people and priests. Living in close proximity with their fellow lay brothers and sisters, they share with them a first hand idea of the Church. They offer them a pattern of life worthy of imitation. They demonstrate that it is possible for lay persons not only for priests and religious to commit themselves to the faith and make sacrifices for it.[137]

58. The Laity and the Mission of Catholic Teaching Institutions

It is impossible to overlook the activity and the service of Catholic educational institutions—of different grades and levels—for the complete formation of new generations of the faithful in Church *communio* and mission. In working together with families and with institutions, they are called to be authentic teaching communities. In these Catholic educational facilities, parents, teachers and students work together professing and spreading the Catholic identity, not only through the actual teaching of religion, but also through participation in cultural and community programs.[138]

59. The Laity: Associations and Movements

Various associations, such as Confraternities, Third Orders, Catholic Action, international Catholic organizations, movements and groups, are indeed valuable forms in Church life of promoting and helping to realize the laity's baptismal dignity and their responsibility to the apostolate. In the variety of their charisms, in their method of teaching Christianity and in their work in the apostolate, they nourish and manifest a real fountainhead of holiness among the *Christifideles*. Such groups provide for conversion and Christian formation, showing themselves to be particularly timely and effective in the Church's mission into the spheres and environments of social activity, that is strongly influenced by secularism and oftentimes inaccessible for parishes.

Nowadays, after the crisis at the end of the 60's, it is possible to speak of a new season for associations among the faithful. While some traditional forms seem to have actually lost importance and others have passed through a process of "updating" in the wake of the conciliar renewal, new groups, communities and Church movements are emerging and spreading with particular vigor.

The novelty and variety of the present season of lay associations requires a process of discernment for the Church, both prudent and timely. In this case, it is impossible to overlook the right to freedom of association amply recognized by the Second Vatican Council [139] and included in the Revised Code of Canon Law.[140] The Council also recommended the promotion of similar forms of association.[141] However, it must be stated that the Bishops, in union with the Pope, have the duty of exercising the delicate work of discerning the charismatic gifts that the Spirit lavishly bestows upon the faithful and which sometimes give rise to forms of association and initiatives in the apostolate.[142]

60. Criteria for Church Associations

It is felt necessary to specify the criteria that guide the growth in the Church of various forms of association without interferring with the work of Bishops in their work of due discernment.

Essentially such criteria for Church associations include faithfulness to the Church magisterium, *communio* with the Pope and the Bishops, and participation in the Church's mission. An important element in evaluating the soundness of such forms or associations are the presence of the fruits of charity, of holiness, of apostolic zeal, of dedication and of service to the Church, as well as the Christian formation of their members in the tasks arising from their vocation.

There is a real concern to increase the bonds of *communio* and participation of associations of the faithful in the local Churches, under the guidance of the Bishops and in *communio* with the Pope and in relation to the programs and institutions of the diocese and to the particular dynamic of "inculturation" in the local situations.

While neither stifling nor forcing the charisms involved in the forms of these associations, their teaching methods, their unique character of work, and in some cases, their international nature—recommended by the Council [143]—the Bishops have the duty to promote *communio* in the Church while directing the contributions of every aspect of Church life toward the common good.

Finally, it is necessary to overcome at the very heart of the Christian community, attitudes of rivalry and conflict, monopoly and exclusion, while promoting in the name of the principle of *communio* a unity in a plurality of forms. Everyone is called to the one and only mission of the Church.

61. CONSECRATED FOR MISSION

Attention must also be given to Secular Institutes and their contribution from their very beginning to the mission of the Church. Indeed, the call which is directed to their members—who are among the laity— to a special consecration according to the evangelical counsels, makes them witnesses in the world of the deep-rooted commitment to a life style based on the gospel. The way of life united with the Christian presence in contemporary society are a sign of the generous response of the laity to the common vocation to perfection in charity. Living their total consecration to God in the world, the lay members of Secular Institutes follow in an exemplary manner that aspect of the Christian vocation which looks to the world to come. Their witness to Christ

Who makes all things new in the world is an encouragement for all the laity to recognize and accept the challenge of "being *in* the world" without "being *of* the world". In virtue of their personal readiness, determined by their state in life, and the formation they experience, many members of Secular Institutes make valid contributions to the human and Christian development of so many other lay faithful, assuming with them important responsibilities in the midst of the Christian community.

This theme merits a particularly thorough consideration. It is impossible on the other hand, to overlook that there is an ever-increasing number of laity deeply committed to the evangelical counsels, but who do not feel called to form or join a Secular Institute. The actual state of Church life is rich with new forms of lay consecrated life, a gift offered to the Church and to the world in our time by the Holy Spirit.

III.

THE FIELDS OF MISSION FOR THE LAITY

62. CRITERIA FOR A RENEWED PRESENCE

Today the laity are called to live in areas which oftentimes are overly secularized. They are called to assume responsibilities in situations and to answer questions which are "pioneer" in character, as well as to cooperate with people of every type of persuasion. For all of these reasons it is necessary that the lay faithful's experience of really belonging to the Church does not cease to grow once they assume a temporal responsibility. This experience of belonging must continually be nourished in the communion of fellowship. There is a need then, to promote in Christian communities an atmosphere more sensitive and attentive to welcoming, listening, consulting and seeking to understand the laity employed in various temporal surroundings.

Christian *communio* by its very nature seeks to permeate all areas of the laity's life in the world with an apostolic presence. Therefore, legitimate diversities reflective of a plurality of choices in social activity, are to be ordered toward the common good and are to seek to avoid a paralysis in effort toward working together with others.[144] In any case the social doctrine of the Church thoroughly studied recently and rooted in a comprehensive anthropology, offers important guidelines for evaluating and directing activity in the world.[145]

The wealth of social doctrine does not provide political models and technical solutions automatically deducible from the Gospel. The Church Herself, whose task of evangelization also includes human development—does not tie her mission to any temporal strategy of defense or to the acquisition of political power. It is the task of the laity, enlightened by faith and educated in social doctrine to invent new ways that lead to solidarity, to the realization of the dignity and to the total development of people and nations.

63. The Christian Presence in the World

Referring to "their own field" and to the "very special form of evangelization" of the laity, the Apostolic Exhortation *Evangelii Nuntiandi* spoke of "the vast and complicated world of politics, society and the arts, of international life, of instruments of social communications and also of other realities, particularly open to evangelization, such as, love, the family, the education of children and adolescents, professional work and suffering".[146] No area of human life or activity can be untouched by the Christian presence. It is a question of evangelizing in an all-pervasive fashion the total range of human experiences.

Nonetheless it is worth highlighting some areas of human existence in which the laity have a primary importance.

64. Urgent Questions

Replies to the *Lineamenta* clearly indicated that many questions on life in today's society are increasingly concerned with problems indiscriminately affecting wide areas of our planet or those seriously threatening specific countries.

In our times a renewed presence of the laity cannot exclude these two urgent questions.

The first series of questions concerns the serious and diverse forms of discrimination and marginalization suffered by many persons or even entire groups of persons as a result of ethnic, social, economic, political, cultural or religious association. While human rights more and more make their impression on the moral conscience of humanity, they are at the same time degraded by authoritarian and totalitarian regimes, by subhuman conditions of survival from a spectre of hunger, by the scandalous continuance of situations of racial discrimination (apartheid), by restrictions and persecutions in the basic area of religious freedom. Christians are in solidarity with the innocent victims of injustice and strive to defend and promote everywhere the dignity of every individual and of all people.[147]

A second series of problems that really concerns people of our time: the search for peace in a world increasingly wounded by violence and tried by war, by terrorism, by torture, by concentration camps and by military interference in politics. The nuclear threat and the arms race weigh heavily on the destiny of humanity. The Church is committed on the front line to the inevitable task of building a peace through conversion of people's "hearts", through the testimony of *communio* and reconciliation and the denunciation of all violent means. The Church knows that peace must be built on the foundation of truth, freedom, justice and charity.[148] The Church is confident that the laity, in collaboration with all those who truly seek peace, might be capable, without irenic illusion, of defeating the culture of hate, vendetta, alienation, and of opening up everywhere glimmerings of truly lived fellowship.[149]

65. The Reality of Marriage and the Family

The family is of decisive importance in the proper well-being of the person and for the soundness of the social framework. Through family life animated from the perspective of Christian holiness, the laity are able to transform daily life and render it more beneficial for the human person both in urban and rural areas.

Fidelity to the indissoluble bond of marriage, respect for the responsibilities of fatherhood and motherhood, the welcome and the support of life, the primary responsibility for the education of children, are the decisive tasks in which an important aspect of the laity's mission is carried out in their everyday labors. The Synod of Bishops' "On the Christian Family in Today's World" and the Apostolic Exhortation *Familiaris Consortio* have amply illustrated the importance of this mission in the Church.[150]

66. THE WORLD OF WORK AND THE ECONOMY

Human work, in its multiple forms, is the key to the social question. For this reason it represents a decisive priority for the mission of the laity.

The dignity of the person and the principle of solidarity are particularly at stake in this area. The importance of giving value to the already existing Christian realities in the world of work and of creating new ones within the workers' movements, among executives and groups in between, appears decisive in light of the deep transformations now taking place in the world of work. Because of the crisis in ideologies it is all the more urgent to rediscover the basic meaning of human work.

In the present phase of world economic development the present systems for the organization of work show themselves incapable of dealing with growing unemployment. Furthermore they continue to hold vast groups of humanity or even entire nations in a state of marginalization through an application of the pure logic of profit, materialism and consumerism that places heavy debts on the shoulders of those who are already poor, representing in miniature the imbalance prevalant in international economics.

The encyclical *Laborem Exercens* [151] offers a perspective and program which deserve a more decisive and creative implementation as the observance of the first centenary of the encyclical *Rerum Novarum* approaches.

67. THE WORLD OF CULTURE AND SCIENCE

The creation and transmission of culture especially constitute for our times one of the principle tasks of social interaction and social evolution. Therefore, the Church must give special pastoral attention to the presence of the laity in schools and universities, in environments of scientific and technological research as well as in the field of the arts and humanities.

The extraordinary discoveries and the immense benefits resulting from science and technology have proved themselves totally insufficient in supplying answers to the profound quest for truth that stirs in the heart of the human person. The crisis in school education is adequate proof. This search for truth and the good of the human person must reassert themselves, particularly in reestablishing the foundation of the social sciences, in deepening the metaphysic of philosophy, in the delicate fields of biogenetic research, information systems, robotics and nuclear energy.

Therefore it is encumbent on all Christians to become more aware of this challenge to the mission of the Church and to the intellectual creativity of the laity.

68. THE WORLD OF SOCIAL COMMUNICATIONS

Rapid innovations, the complex development and far-reaching influence in formation of a mentality to dominate, make the world of the "mass media" a new frontier for the mission of the Church. In particular, the responsibility of professionals in this field among the laity, whether exercised personally or through the promotion of initiatives arising from Christian institutions, requires that all its inherent value be acknowledged and supported through more adequate material, intellectual and pastoral resources.[152]

There is an unprecedented urgency for education in a critical sense, motivated by a passion for the truth, regarding the use and reception of these powerful instruments of communication. In the mass-media field the laity must be defenders of freedom, respect for the dignity of the human person and the growth of an authentic culture of peoples. They are to reject every form of monopolizing and manipulation, especially the extolling of hatred, violence, eroticism, unchecked consumerism, and the break up of moral values for the person and the family.

69. The World of Politics

The dignity and rights of the human person along with the responsible participation of citizens in public affairs are the pivotal points of an authentic political activity. For the laity, involvement in political life ought to be considered as a particularly binding obligation in charity which seeks the service of others in light of the common good.[153]

A skeptical attitude to "politics" has no reasonable foundation among Christians. However, they ought to react against every manifestation of idolatry and cynicism toward "power". It seems particularly important to promote among the laity's vocations, a political involvement which places Christian values at the service of the human person and the progress of justice in the life among nations. The development of international institutions cannot be overlooked in the programs of Christians.[154] Even though an individual Christian's political choices involve only personal or group responsibility and do not represent the whole Church, Christian communities and their Bishops are to be near at hand and kindly disposed to people in politics with the view of helping them truly live their sensitive responsibility in deep unity with their faith.

IV.
THE FORMATION OF THE LAITY

70. The Necessity for Formation

Growth in the spiritual life and the commitment for mission require that the laity receive a well grounded and complete formation, offered by the Church in a variety of ways and at different stages of life.

A distinction must be made between a basic working catechesis and various types of a more specialized continuing formation. The laity's formation ought to be seen as an education to discovering, deepening and developing their proper Christian vocation and mission. Therefore, this formation, if it is to be a complete program of education, must go beyond the mere teaching of theory and have as its starting point a truly experiential life in the Church. Supported by the witness of Christian saints, this formation progressively brings to life a growing awareness of the meaning of belonging to the Church community.

Formation must not neglect giving careful consideration to the importance of the various surroundings in which the laity find themselves.

71. TOTAL FORMATION

The whole purpose of formation is the growth of the Christian life in all its aspects, so that the laity may acquire the knowledge and dispositions needed to bring their spiritual life to maturity and to fulfill their tasks in the apostolate. Formation must be complete because the Christian life is an organic unity. To neglect any one of its aspects is to bring harm to all the others. There is need therefore to develop a knowledge of faith, participation in the sacraments and liturgy, and the workings of charity, all in a harmonious manner.

72. THE PERSONAL DEEPENING OF VOCATION

Formation is particularly important during infancy and adolescence, for it is in this period that the different choices of life develop. From the period of infancy, every believer should learn to discern the call of God, which indicates where the divine plan of salvation is to be realized.

The laity need to be increasingly aware that to follow Christ in the secular life truly constitutes an authentic Christian vocation.

This vocation also includes the mission of bearing witness to Christ in the very heart of human society,[155] in addition to breathing the Christian spirit into every earthly reality for the glory of God and the salvation of the world.

A well grounded spiritual and catechetical formation ought to know how to show that the choice of marriage is a substantial aspect of the Christian vocation for many lay women and men.[156] Indeed, in marriage spouses are called to holiness. By God's design, conjugal love becomes a part of the realization of the work of redemption. The Christian family becomes the domestic church, the dwelling of faith and charity.

Another vocation worthy of great esteem is that of the laity who choose to remain unmarried so as to dedicate their whole life to the mission of caring for other lay Christians.

Furthermore, the laity ought to know that in this world God calls to a special union with the crucified Christ all those who are oppressed by poverty, bodily weakness, sickness and troubles of mind, or who suffer persecution for justice' sake. Such suffering is of great value for the good of the world; and after this brief time of suffering God Himself will lead them to perfection bringing them to eternal security and wholeness.[157]

73. THE BASIC IMPORTANCE OF CATECHESIS

From the earliest days of the Church, catechesis has always been the foundation of coming to know the tenets of the Faith. It has always had an organic relationship with the sacraments of initiation, both as a preparation for Baptism and in the process of deepening the Baptismal vocation. Such a catechesis introduces the laity to all aspects of the Mystery of Christ and life in the Church, opening them to the full sense of the Christian identity, with all its privileges and demands.[158]

In the catechetical formation of the laity it is necessary to bear in mind the specific character of their way of fulfilling their vocation. Communication is needed to instill in them a knowledge and disposition that will help them bring their Christian faith to bear on all the situations which form the fabric of their lives, above all those situations of family, work, culture, social and political life.[159]

74. CONTINUING FORMATION

It would be most beneficial if the laity reach a level of Christian formation which corresponds to the level of their cultural surroundings in the world. Otherwise they run the risk of a dangerous imbalance:

their faith dries up and they are no longer capable of fulfilling their mission.

For this reason the Bishops of the Church ought to be concerned in providing the opportunity for continuing formation which would enrich them in various fields (biblical, theological, moral, liturgical and spiritual). Thus the laity will be able to respond to their social, economic and political responsibilities in a Christian spirit and inculturate the gospel into the various situations of their daily lives.

Particular attention is required in the formation of the laity in the social teaching of the Church, until that moment when that civilization of truth and love which the Church wishes to promote becomes fulfilled. The laity are to contribute in a creative manner to the development of this doctrine and to its application for the good of society as a whole.

75. The Importance of Popular Forms of Religion

Guided by the Spirit and by the Church's teaching, the laity in many countries have known how to give a living expression to the faith, both spontaneous and popular. This is witnessed in customs and language, in devotions and feasts, in the stream of pilgrims to certain sanctuaries, in the art and Christian wisdom of people. This inculturation of the faith at work through the centuries, is welcomed with respect and encouraged. The eventual shortcomings or defects that can appear in these manifestations find a remedy in a catechetical effort aimed at strengthening the appreciation of the faith (*sensus fidei*) among the people.

76. The Laity in the Formation of Others

Many laity, women and men, generously assume the task of forming other members of the faithful. By means of lessons, lectures and series of conferences on subjects in which they have professional competence, they can offer Christian solutions to many current problems. Above all in catechesis, in spiritual counsel, in the service of Church communities that lack ordained ministers, their task of formation takes on very special importance.

These lay men and women deserve assurances of a formation more complete and more deeply personal because in addition to seeking to conform their lives to the gospel, they are attempting to share with other Christians a response to their questions and problems.

Therefore, they are in need of a spiritual life firmly rooted in Christ and in a deep sense of dedication to the Church. They are to make sure that they cooperate sincerely with the Bishops of the Church and be prepared to share with them their experiences, the progress achieved and the difficulties encountered. On the other hand, they are to be truly open to the needs of others, ready to serve them, while avoiding every attitude which does not correspond to Christian humility.

77. PRIESTS AND THE FORMATION OF THE LAITY

Various replies to the *Lineamenta* have underlined the necessity for all priests to encourage the advancement of the laity, according to the impetus given by the Second Vatican Council. First of all priests ought to contribute to the formation of the laity, fully respecting their own vocation and resisting the temptation to clericalize them or to exclude them.

Since "among the other gifts of God which are found abundantly among the faithful, special attention ought to be devoted to those graces by which a considerable number of people are attracted to greater heights of the spiritual life",[160] priests are to help the laity to grow in the spiritual life through a personal union with Christ in their daily life and participation in the life of the entire community.

Furthermore, "in testing the spirits to see if they be of God, the clergy must discover with faith, recognize with joy, and foster with diligence the many and varied charismatic gifts of the laity, whether these be of a humble or a more exalted kind".[161]

They are to exercise great care for the formation of the laity in the apostolate, pointing out the importance of their mission for the Christian transformation of the world and the good of the entire family of humanity.

For the general Christian formation of all the People of God, preaching, especially the Sunday homily, has a decisive importance for the continuing education in the faith. Priests, therefore, are to strive to give a proper care to their preaching in which they are to emphasize strongly in a suitable manner the excellence of the vocation and mission of the laity in the Church and in the world.

Today, formation programs for candidates to the priesthood must put a greater emphasis on serving the needs of the laity and working together with them. Indeed, future priests are to become generous "examples to the flock" (1 Peter 5:3), being in the midst of the laity as the Lord Jesus, who "came not to be served but to serve, and to give His life as a ransom for many" (Mt 20:28). In this way these men will bear witness to the richness of a life in Christ and will join their efforts to those of the laity, united together in accomplishing the one and only mission of the Church.[162]

CONCLUSION

78. In the Church and in the World

Twenty years after the close of the Second Vatican Council, the situation of the laity in the Church and in the world reflects the Council's fruitfulness and engenders hope in still further progress.

In the Church, the laity's vocation and mission has been acknowledged in a more explicit and effective way. In fact, the ecclesiology of *communio,* "a central and fundamental concept of the Council documents",[163] provides an understanding to every aspect of Church life, revealing that through *communio* "there is a common dignity of members, deriving from their rebirth in Christ, a common grace as His children, a common vocation to perfection".[164] Precisely for this reason many lay women and men have become more aware of the magnitude of their vocation. They are conscious of having been called personally by God the Father to live as His child, in fellowship with others, through the love of Christ and *communio* with the Holy Spirit. From this perspective they give generously of themselves, with a growing sense of responsibility, to the various expressions of Church life, both in its internal growth and in its external works in the apostolate.

In the present world, the situation of the laity is certainly not easy. In fact, serious and widespread problems are not lacking. Hunger, oppression and war reduce a part of humanity to an inhuman lot, while, in a contrary sense, the abundance of material and cultural goods pose dangers of a different but no less fearful variety. Nevertheless, even in such conditions promises, founded on the exercise of *communio,* provide encouragement. Indeed, if the hope of solution for the grave problems of the world exists, it is found in the dynamisms of participation which now take on a totally new depth and vigor, even if they sometimes diminish, or take false directions. In the ecclesiology of *communio,* the laity find incomparable resources to enable them to meet the expectations of the world and courageously to cure its ills. Their mission consists in spreading divine charity everywhere, communicated in remaining close to Christ in faith, and of drawing men and women of our time to the *communio* which God offers to all in the Church of Christ.

These points for reflection and meditation are submitted to the Fathers of the Seventh Ordinary General Assembly of the Synod of Bishops, so that, recognizing the vocation and mission of the disciples of Christ based on the teachings of the Second Vatican Council, they can effectively be able to demonstrate to the laity the way that leads to that *communio* "with the Father and with his Son" (*1 John* 1:3), in which they have gained entrance through the Holy Spirit, the Lord and Giver of Life.[165]

NOTAE

¹ SYNODI EPISCOPORUM *De vocatione et missione laicorum in Ecclesia et in mundo:* ...
Lineamenta (1985), n. 12.

PARS I

² Cfr. IOANNIS PAULI II *Alloc. ad Sodales Consilii Secretariae Generalis Synodi Episcoporum* (19-5-1984), 4: *AAS* 76 (1984) 785.
³ Cfr. CONC. OEC. VAT. II Const. dogm. de Ecclesia *Lumen Gentium,* 31: *AAS* 57 (1965) 37.
⁴ Cfr. CONC. OEC. VAT. II Const. past. de Ecclesia in mundo huius temporis *Gaudium et Spes,* 10: *AAS* 58 (1966) 1033.
⁵ Cfr. CONC. OEC. VAT. II Decr. de apostolatu Laicorum *Apostolicam Actuositatem,* 19: *AAS* 58 (1966) 854; *Codicis Iuris Canonici,* can. 215.
⁶ Cfr. SYNODI EPISCOPORUM *Relationis finalis extraordinarii coetus generalis II* (8-12-85), II C 1.

PARS II

⁷ Cfr. CONC. OEC. VAT. II Decr. de apostolatu Laicorum *Apostolicam Actuositatem,* 1: *AAS* 58 (1966) 837.
⁸ Cfr. SYNODI EPISCOPORUM *Relationis finalis extraordinarii coetus generalis II* (8-12-1985), II C 1.
⁹ Cfr. CONC. OEC. VAT. II Const. dogm. de Ecclesia *Lumen Gentium,* 39: *AAS* 57 (1965) 44.
¹⁰ Cfr. *Io* 17, 26; *2 Cor* 13, 13.
¹¹ Cfr. CONC. OEC. VAT. II Const. dogm. de Ecclesia *Lumen Gentium,* 31: *AAS* 57 (1965) 37.
¹² Cfr. *Gen* 1, 28.
¹³ Cfr. CONC. OEC. VAT. II Const. past. de Ecclesia in mundo huius temporis *Gaudium et Spes,* 34: *AAS* 58 (1966) 1053.
¹⁴ Cfr. *ibid.* 50: *AAS* 58 (1966) 1071.
¹⁵ Cfr. *ibid.* 34: *AAS* 58 (1966) 1052.
¹⁶ Cfr. IOANNIS PAULI II *Epist. Apost. Salvifici Doloris,* 19: AAS 76 (1984) 225-226.
¹⁷ Cfr. *Mt* 5, 11 ss.; *1 Pet* 4, 14.
¹⁸ Cfr. *1 Pet* 1, 15.
¹⁹ Cfr. CONC. OEC. VAT. II Decr. de Oecumenismo *Unitatis Redintegratio,* 2: *AAS* 57 (1965) 91.
²⁰ Cfr. *Io* 17, 21-23.
²¹ Cfr. *Gen* 1, 31.
²² Cfr. CONC. OEC. VAT. II Const. past. de Ecclesia in mundo huius temporis *Gaudium et Spes,* 39: *AAS* 58 (1966) 1056-1057.
²³ CONC. OEC. VAT. II Const. dogm. de Ecclesia *Lumen Gentium,* 5: *AAS* 57 (1965) 8.
²⁴ Cfr. *1 Io* 1, 3.

[25] Cfr. Conc. Oec. Vat. II Const. past. de Ecclesia in mundo huius temporis *Gaudium et Spes*, 13: *AAS* 58 (1966) 1034-1035.

[26] Cfr. Conc. Oec. Vat. II Decr. de Oecumenismo *Unitatis Redintegratio*, 12: *AAS* 57 (1965) 99-100.

[27] Cfr. Conc. Oec. Vat. II Const. past. de Ecclesia in mundo huius temporis *Gaudium et Spes*, 93: *AAS* 58 (1966) 1114.

[28] Cfr. *Rom* 6, 3-5; *1 Cor* 12, 12-13; Conc. Oec. Vat. II Const. dogm. de Ecclesia *Lumen Gentium*, 31: *AAS* 57 (1965) 37.

[29] Cfr. *Rom* 14, 7-8; *2 Cor* 5, 15; *Gal* 2, 19-20.

[30] Cfr. *Io* 15, 9.

[31] Cfr. *Eph* 4, 5.

[32] Cfr. Conc. Oec. Vat. II Const. dogm. de Ecclesia *Lumen Gentium*, 32: *AAS* 57 (1965) 38; Decr. de Presbyterorum ministerio et vita *Presbyterorum Ordinis* 9: *AAS* 58 (1966) 1005.

[33] Synodi Episcoporum *Relationis finalis extraordinarii coetus generalis II* (8-12-85), II D 1; Conc. Oec. Vat. II Const. dogm. de Ecclesia *Lumen Gentium*, 48: *AAS* 57 (1965) 53.

[34] Cfr. Codicis Iuris Canonici, can. 217.

[35] Cfr. Conc. Oec. Vat. II Const. dogm. de Ecclesia *Lumen Gentium*, 11: *AAS* 57 (1965) 15.

[36] Cfr. Conc. Oec. Vat. II Decr. de apostolatu Laicorum *Apostolicam Actuositatem*, 3: *AAS* 58 (1966) 839.

[37] Cfr. Codicis Iuris Canonici, can. 216.

[38] Cfr. *ibid.*, can. 215.

[39] Cfr. *ibid.*, can. 223, 2.

[40] Cfr. *1 Cor* 10, 17; *Rom* 12, 5; Conc. Oec. Vat. II Const. dogm. de Ecclesia *Lumen Gentium*, 7: *AAS* 57 (1965) 10; Ioannis Pauli II Epist. *Dominicae Cenae*, 4: *AAS* 72 (1980) 119-121.

[41] Ruperti T. *De Divinis Officiis*, II, 11: Migne, *PL* 170, 43.

[42] Cfr. *Mt* 26, 28; *Eph* 1, 7.

[43] Cfr. Ioannis Pauli II Adhort. Apost. *Reconciliatio et Paenitentia*, 28: *AAS* 77 (1985) 250 ss.

[44] Cfr. Ioannis Pauli II Litt. Enc. *Redemptor Hominis*, 20: *AAS* 71 (1979) 313.

[45] Cfr. Conc. Oec. Vat. II Const. dogm. de Ecclesia *Lumen Gentium*, 31: *AAS* 57 (1965) 37; Decr. de apostolatu Laicorum *Apostolicam Actuositatem*, 2: *AAS* 58 (1966) 838-839.

[46] Cfr. Conc. Oec. Vat. II Decr. de apostolatu Laicorum *Apostolicam Actuositatem*, 3: *AAS* 58 (1966) 839.

[47] Cfr. *1 Pet* 2, 5; *Apoc* 1, 6; 5, 10.

[48] Cfr. Conc. Oec. Vat. II Const. dogm. de Ecclesia *Lumen Gentium*, 10. 34: *AAS* 57 (1965) 14. 40.

[49] *Ibid.*, 12, p. 16.

[50] *Ibid.*, 35, p. 40.

[51] Cfr. *Io* 12, 32; *1 Cor* 15, 28.

[52] Cfr. Conc. Oec. Vat. II Const. dogm. de Ecclesia *Lumen Gentium*, 36: *AAS* 57 (1965) 41; Ioannis Pauli II Litt. Enc. *Redemptor Hominis*, 21: *AAS* 71 (1979) 316.

[53] Cfr. Conc. Oec. Vat. II Const. dogm. de Ecclesia *Lumen Gentium*, 37: *AAS* 57 (1965) 43.

[54] Ex *Hymno akathisto*: Migne, *PG* 92, 1338, 35-39.

[55] Cfr. *Lc* 1, 38; *Io* 19, 26-27; Ioannis Pauli II Litt. Enc. *Redemptor Hominis*, 22: *AAS* 71 (1979) 323.

[56] Cfr. Ioannis Pauli II *Alloc. in Urbe Tegucigalpa (Honduras)* (8-3-1983), 6: *AAS* 75 (1983) 753-754.

[57] Cfr. Conc. Oec. Vat. II Const. past. de Ecclesia in mundo huius temporis *Gaudium et Spes*, 60: *AAS* 58 (1966) 1081; Decr. de apostolatu Laicorum *Apostolicam Actuositatem*, 4: *AAS* 58 (1966) 841.

⁵⁸ Cfr. Conc. Oec. Vat. II Const. dogm. de Ecclesia *Lumen Gentium*, 33: *AAS* 57 (1965) 39; Decr. de apostolatu Laicorum *Apostolicam Actuositatem*, 3: *AAS* 58 (1966) 839.

⁵⁹ Cfr. *Rom* 6, 11.

⁶⁰ Cfr. *1 Cor* 12, 4-6.

⁶¹ Cfr. Conc. Oec. Vat. II Const. dogm. de Ecclesia *Lumen Gentium*, 12: *AAS* 57 (1965) 16; Decr. de apostolatu Laicorum *Apostolicam Actuositatem*, 3: *AAS* 58 (1966) 839.

⁶² Cfr. Synodi Episcoporum *Relationis finalis extraordinarii coetus generalis II* (8-2-85), II D 3.

⁶³ Cfr. Conc. Oec. Vat. II Const. past. de Ecclesia in mundo huius temporis *Gaudium et Spes*, 43: *AAS* 58 (1966) 1062-1063.

⁶⁴ Cfr. Conc. Oec. Vat. II Const. dogm. de Ecclesia *Lumen Gentium*, 31: *AAS* 57 (1965) 38.

⁶⁵ Cfr. Synodi Episcoporum *Relationis finalis extraordinarii coetus generalis II* (8-12-85), II D 2 et 3.

⁶⁶ *Ibid.* II D 6.

⁶⁷ Cfr. Conc. Oec. Vat. II Const. past. de Ecclesia in mundo huius temporis *Gaudium et Spes*, 43: *AAS* 58 (1966) 1062; Decr. de apostolatu Laicorum *Apostolicam Actuositatem*, 7: *AAS* 58 (1966) 844.

⁶⁸ *Ibid.* 5: *AAS* 58 (1966) 842; Congr. pro Doctrina Fidei Instr. de libertate christiana et liberatione *Libertatis Conscientiae* (22-3-1986), 80.

⁶⁹ Cfr. Conc. Oec. Vat. II Const. dogm. de Ecclesia *Lumen Gentium*, 11: *AAS* 57 (1965) 15-16.

⁷⁰ Cfr. *Eph* 5, 21-23; Ioannis Pauli II Adhort. Apost. *Familiaris Consortio*, 13: *AAS* 74 (1982) 95.

⁷¹ *Ibid.* 11: *AAS* 74 (1982) 91-93.

⁷² Cfr. Conc. Oec. Vat. II Const. dogm. de Ecclesia *Lumen Gentium*, 11: *AAS* 57 (1965) 16; Decr. de apostolatu Laicorum *Apostolicam Actuositatem*, 11: *AAS* 58 (1966) 848.

⁷³ Cfr. Conc. Oec. Vat. II Const. past. de Ecclesia in mundo huius temporis *Gaudium et Spes*, 48: *AAS* 58 (1966) 1067.

⁷⁴ Conc. Oec. Vat. II Const. dogm. de Ecclesia *Lumen Gentium*, 35: *AAS* 57 (1965) 41.

⁷⁵ Cfr. *1 Cor* 12, 4-11. 28-31; *Rom* 12, 6-8; *1 Pet* 4, 10-11.

⁷⁶ Cfr. Conc. Oec. Vat. II Const. dogm. de Ecclesia *Lumen Gentium*, 4. 12. 25. 30: *AAS* 57 (1965) 6 s. 16 s. 29 ss. 37; Decr. de apostolatu Laicorum *Apostolicam Actuositatem*, 3: *AAS* 58 (1966) 839 s.; Decr. de activitate missionali Ecclesiae *Ad Gentes*, 4, 28: *AAS* 58 (1966) 950 s. 979.

⁷⁷ Cfr. Conc. Oec. Vat. II Decr. de apostolatu Laicorum *Apostolicam Actuositatem*, 3: *AAS* 58 (1966) 839.

⁷⁸ *Ibid.* 3: *AAS* 58 (1966) 840.

⁷⁹ Cfr. Conc. Oec. Vat. II Const. dogm. de Ecclesia *Lumen Gentium*, 12: *AAS* 57 (1965) 17.

⁸⁰ *Ibid.* 7: *AAS* 57 (1965) 10.

⁸¹ *Ibid.* 12: *AAS* 57 (1965) 17.

⁸² *Ibid.* 30: *AAS* 57 (1965) 37.

⁸³ *Ibid.* 33: *AAS* 57 (1965) 39.

⁸⁴ Cfr. Pauli VI Adhort. Apost. *Evangelii Nuntiandi*, 73: *AAS* 68 (1976) 61-63; Litt. Apost. *Ministeria Quaedam: AAS* 64 (1972) 529-534.

⁸⁵ Ioannis Pauli II *Alloc. ad laicos in urbe Fulda: Insegnamenti* III, 2 (1980) 1299-1310.

⁸⁶ Cfr. Pauli VI Adhort. Apost. *Evangelii Nuntiandi*, 73: *AAS* 68 (1976) 62.

⁸⁷ Cfr. Ioannis Pauli II *Alloc. ad clerum Helveticum, in urbe Einsiedeln: AAS* 77 (1985) 63.

⁸⁸ Conc. Trid. sess. XXIV, *Decr. de sacram. matrimonii*, can. 10: Denz.-Schönm. 1810.

[89] Cfr. CONC. OEC. VAT. II Const. past. de Ecclesia in mundo huius temporis *Gaudium et Spes,* 43: *AAS* 58 (1966) 1062-1063.

[90] Cfr. CONC. OEC. VAT. II Const. dogm. de Ecclesia *Lumen Gentium,* 40: *AAS* 57 (1965) 44.

[91] Cfr. *Rom* 6, 2-4.

[92] Cfr. *1 Io* 2, 6.

[93] Cfr. *Heb* 10, 5-10.

[94] Cfr. *Mt* 16, 22-24.

[95] Cfr. *Mt* 25, 31-46.

[96] Cfr. CONGR. PRO DOCTRINA FIDEI Instr. de libertate christiana et liberatione *Libertatis Conscientiae* (22-3-1986), 62.

[97] Cfr. CONC. OEC. VAT. II Decr. de apostolatu Laicorum *Apostolicam Actuositatem,* 4: *AAS* 58 (1966) 840-841.

[98] Cfr. *Mt* 13, 31-32.

[99] Cfr. CONC. OEC. VAT. II Const. dogm. de Divina Revelatione *Dei Verbum,* 21: *AAS* 58 (1966) 827-828.

[100] *Ibid.* 828.

[101] Cfr. CONC. OEC. VAT. II Decr. de apostolatu Laicorum *Apostolicam Actuositatem,* 4: *AAS* 58 (1966) 840.

[102] Cfr. CONC. OEC. VAT. II Const. dogm. de Ecclesia *Lumen Gentium,* 11: *AAS* 57 (1965) 15.

[103] Cfr. *ibid.* 34: *AAS* 57 (1965) 40.

[104] Cfr. *Lc* 18, 1; 22, 40; *Rom* 12, 12.

[105] Cfr. CONC. OEC. VAT. II Decr. de Oecumenismo *Unitatis Redintegratio,* 3: *AAS* 57 (1965) 94.

[106] CONC. OEC. VAT. II Decr. de Presbyterorum ministerio et vita *Presbyterorum Ordinis,* 5: *AAS* 58 (1966) 998.

[107] Cfr. *2 Pet* 3, 9.

[108] Cfr. *Lc* 15, 22-24.

[109] Cfr. *1 Cor* 9, 25-27.

[110] CONC. OEC. VAT. II Const. dogm. de Ecclesia *Lumen Gentium,* 41: *AAS* 57 (1965) 45.

[111] Cfr. CONC. OEC. VAT. II Decr. de apostolatu Laicorum *Apostolicam Actuositatem,* 4: *AAS* 58 (1966) 841.

[112] *Ibid.*

[113] CONC. OEC. VAT. II Const. dogm. de Ecclesia *Lumen Gentium,* 62: *AAS* 57 (1965) 63.

[114] *Ibid.* 35: *AAS* 57 (1965) 41.

[115] Cfr. PAULI VI Adhort. Apost. *Evangelii Nuntiandi,* 14: *AAS* 68 (1976) 13.

[116] SYNODI EPISCOPORUM *Relationis finalis extraordinarii coetus generalis II* (8-12-1985), II D 4; IOANNIS PAULI II, Epist. Enc. *Slavorum Apostoli* 18, 19, 21: *AAS* 77 (1985) 800-803.

[117] Cfr. *Lc* 2, 52.

[118] Cfr. CONC. OEC. VAT. II Decr. de apostolatu Laicorum *Apostolicam Actuositatem,* 9: *AAS* 58 (1966) 846.

[119] Cfr. CONC. OEC. VAT. II Const. past. de Ecclesia in mundo huius temporis *Gaudium et Spes,* 1: AAS 58 (1966) 1025.

[120] Cfr. IOANNIS PAULI II Epist. Apost. *Salvifici Doloris,* 31: *AAS* 75 (1984) 250.

[121] Cfr. CONC. OEC. VAT. II Const. past. de Ecclesia in mundo huius temporis *Gaudium et Spes,* 1: *AAS* 58 (1966) 1025-1026.

[122] IOANNIS PAULI II Litt. Enc. *Redemptor Hominis,* 21: *AAS* 71 (1979) 320.

[123] Cfr. CONC. OEC. VAT. II Const. past. de Ecclesia in mundo huius temporis *Gaudium et Spes,* 41: *AAS* 58 (1966) 1059; IOANNIS PAULI II Litt. Enc. *Redemptor Hominis,* 8, 10: *AAS* 71 (1979) 271, 274.

[124] Congr. pro Doctrina Fidei Instr. de libertate christiana et liberatione *Libertatis Conscientiae* (22-3-1986), 71.

[125] Cfr. *Act* 4, 13. 29-31: «parrhesia».

[126] Cfr. Conc. Oec. Vat. II Decr. de activitate missionali Ecclesiae *Ad Gentes*, 11: *AAS* 58 (1966) 959; Const. dogm. de Ecclesia *Lumen Gentium*, 38: *AAS* 57 (1965) 43.

[127] Cfr. Conc. Oec. Vat. II Const. past. de Ecclesia in mundo huius temporis *Gaudium et Spes*, 39: *AAS* 58 (1966) 1056; Const. dogm. de Ecclesia *Lumen Gentium*, 48: *AAS* 57 (1965) 53.

[128] Cfr. Pauli VI Adhort. Apost. *Evangelii Nuntiandi*, 60: *AAS* 68 (1976) 50-51.

[129] Cfr. Conc. Oec. Vat. II Decr. de Oecumenismo *Unitatis Redintegratio*, 5. 24: *AAS* 57 (1965) 96. 107.

[130] Cfr. Conc. Oec. Vat. II Declar. de Ecclesiae habitudine ad Religiones non-Christianas *Nostra Aetate*, 2: *AAS* 58 (1966) 741; Ioannis Pauli II Litt. Enc. *Redemptor Hominis*, 6: *AAS* 71 (1979) 262-268.

[131] Cfr. Conc. Oec. Vat. II Const. past. de Ecclesia in mundo huius temporis *Gaudium et Spes*, 92: *AAS* 58 (1966) 1114; Decr. de activitate missionali Ecclesiae *Ad Gentes*, 11: *AAS* 58 (1966) 959-960.

[132] Cfr. Pauli VI Litt. Enc. *Populorum Progressio*, 20, 21: *AAS* 59 (1967) 267-268.

[133] Cfr. Conc. Oec. Vat. II Const. dogm. de Ecclesia *Lumen Gentium*, 23. 26. 27: *AAS* 57 (1965) 27. 31. 32.

[134] Cfr. Conc. Oec. Vat. II Decr. de pastorali Episcoporum munere in Ecclesia *Christus Dominus*, 27: *AAS* 58 (1966) 687.

[135] Cfr. Conc. Oec. Vat. II Decr. de apostolatu Laicorum *Apostolicam Actuositatem*, 10: *AAS* 58 (1966) 846; Ioannis Pauli Adhort. Apost. *Catechesi Tradendae*, 67: *AAS* 71 (1979) 1332.

[136] Cfr. Pauli VI Adhort. Apost. *Evangelii Nuntiandi*, 58: *AAS* 68 (1976) 46-49; Congr. pro Doctrina Fidei Instr. de libertate christiana et liberatione *Libertatis Conscientiae* (22-3-1986), 68.

[137] Ioannis Pauli II *Alloc. ad catechistas in urbe Kaduna: Insegnamenti* V, 1 (1982) 432.

[138] Congr. per l'Educazione Cattolica, *Il laico cattolico testimone della fede nella scuola*, Roma 1982.

[139] Cfr. Conc. Oec. Vat. II Const. dogm. de Ecclesia *Lumen Gentium*, 37: *AAS* 57 (1965) 43; Decr. de apostolatu Laicorum *Apostolicam Actuositatem*, 18-20: *AAS* 58 (1966) 852-855.

[140] Cfr. *Codicis Iuris Canonici*, cann. 215-216, 298-329.

[141] Cfr. Conc. Oec. Vat. II Decr. de apostolatu Laicorum *Apostolicam Actuositatem*, 21: *AAS* 58 (1966) 855.

[142] Cfr. Conc. Oec. Vat. II Const. dogm. de Ecclesia *Lumen Gentium*, 12: *AAS* 57 (1965) 16-17; Decr. de apostolatu Laicorum *Apostolicam Actuositatem*, 3: *AAS* 58 (1966) 839; Decr. de Persbyterorum ministerio et vita *Presbyterorum Ordinis*, 9: *AAS* 58 (1966) 1006.

[143] Cfr. Conc. Oec. Vat. II Decr. de apostolatu Laicorum *Apostolicam Actuositatem*, 19, 21: *AAS* 58 (1966) 853, 855; Const. past. de Ecclesia in mundo huius temporis *Gaudium et Spes*, 90: *AAS* 58 (1966) 1112; Decr. de activitate missionali Ecclesiae *Ad Gentes*, 41: *AAS* 58 (1966) 988-989.

[144] Congr. pro Doctrina Fidei Instr. de libertate christiana et liberatione *Libertatis Conscientiae* (22-3-1986), 80.

[145] In praefata Instructione de libertate christiana et liberatione praebetur elenchus ordinatus rerum quae ad Doctrinam socialem Ecclesiae pertinent, nn. 71-96.

[146] Cfr. Pauli VI Adhort. Apost. *Evangelii Nuntiandi*, 70: *AAS* 68 (1976) 60.

[147] Cfr. Conc. Oec. Vat. II Const. past. de Ecclesia in mundo huius temporis *Gaudium et Spes*, 1: *AAS* 58 (1966) 1025; Declar. de Ecclesiae habitudine ad Religiones non-Christianas *Nostra Aetate*, 5: *AAS* 58 (1966) 743-744; Ioannis Pauli II Litt. Enc. *Redemptor Hominis*, 17: *AAS* 71 (1979) 295-300.

[148] Cfr. IOANNIS XXIII Litt. Enc. de pace omnium gentium in veritate, iustitia, caritate, libertate constituenda *Pacem in Terris: AAS* 55 (1963) 257-304.

[149] Cfr. CONC. OEC. VAT. II Const. past. de Ecclesia in mundo huius temporis *Gaudium et Spes*, 77-90: *AAS* 58 (1966) 1100-1112; Nuntios ob diem ad pacem fovendam Calendis ianuariis celebrandum 1968-1987.

[150] IOANNIS PAULI II Adhort. Apost. *Familiaris Consortio: AAS* 74 (1982) 81-192.

[151] IOANNIS PAULI II Litt. Enc. *Laborem Exercens: AAS* 73 (1981) 577-647.

[152] Cfr. CONC. OEC. VAT. II Decr. de instrumentis communicationis socialis *Inter Mirifica*, 13-22: *AAS* 56 (1964) 149-152; Nuntios ob diem ad rectum usum fovendum instrumentorum Communicationis Socialis statutum 1968-1986.

[153] Cfr. CONC. OEC. VAT. II Const. past. de Ecclesia in mundo huius temporis *Gaudium et Spes*, 73-76: *AAS* 58 (1966) 1094-1100.

[154] *Ibid*. 88-90: *AAS* 58 (1966) 1111-1112.

[155] *Ibid*. 43: *AAS* 58 (1966) 1063.

[156] Cfr. IOANNIS PAULI II Adhort. Apost. *Familiaris Consortio*, 66: *AAS* 74 (1982) 159-162.

[157] Cfr. *1 Pet* 5, 10; CONC. OEC. VAT. II Const. dogm. de Ecclesia *Lumen Gentium*, 41: *AAS* 57 (1965) 47.

[158] Cfr. *Directorium catechisticum generale*, 21.

[159] *Ibid*. 26.

[160] CONC. OEC. VAT. II Decr. de Presbyterorum ministerio et vita *Presbyterorum Ordinis* 9: *AAS* 58 (1966) 1006;

[161] *Ibid*.

[162] Cfr. *ibid*., pp. 1005-1006; Decr. de apostolatu Laicorum *Apostolicam Actuositatem*, 6: *AAS* 58 (1966) 842.

CONCLUSIO

[163] SYNODI EPISCOPORUM *Relationis finalis extraordinarii coetus generalis II* (8-12-85), II C 1.

[164] CONC. OEC. VAT. II Const. dogm. de Ecclesia *Lumen Gentium*, 32: *AAS* 57 (1965) 38.

[165] Cfr. IOANNIS PAULI II Litt. Enc. *Dominum et Vivificantem*, 52. 1: *AAS* 78 (1986) 872-874. 809.